How to Become a Highly Paid Internet Joint Venture Broker

I0473812

Paul Marlow

ISBN 10: 1470092298
ISBN 13: 978-1470092290

First Printing, 2012

Printed in the United States of America

Income Disclaimer

This book contains business strategies, marketing methods and other business advice that, regardless of my own results and experience, may not produce the same results (or any results) for you. I make absolutely no guarantee, expressed or implied, that by following the advice below you will make any money or improve current profits, as there are several factors and variables that come into play regarding any given business.

Primarily, results will depend on the nature of the product or business model, the conditions of the marketplace, the experience of the individual, and situations and elements that are beyond your control.

As with any business endeavor, you assume all risk related to investment and money based on your own discretion and at your own potential expense.

Liability Disclaimer

To the fullest extent permitted by law, the sellers are providing this written material, its subsidiary elements and its contents on an 'as is' basis and make no (and expressly disclaim all) representations or warranties of any kind with respect to this material or its contents including, without limitation, advice and recommendations, warranties or merchantability and fitness for a particular purpose. The information is given for entertainment purposes only. In addition, we do not represent or warrant that the information accessible via this material is accurate, complete or current. To the fullest extent permitted by law, neither the sellers or any of its affiliates, partners, directors, employees or other representatives will be liable for damages arising out of or in connection with the use of this material. This is a comprehensive limitation of liability that applies to all damages of any kind, including (without limitation) compensatory, direct, indirect or consequential damages, loss of data, income or profit, loss of or damage to property and claims of third parties.

By reading this book, you assume all risks associated with using the advice given below, with a full understanding that you, solely, are responsible for anything that may occur as a result of putting this information into action in any way, and regardless of your interpretation of the advice.

You further agree that our company cannot be held responsible in any way for the success or failure of your business as a result of the information presented in this book. It is your responsibility to conduct your own due diligence regarding the safe and successful operation of your business if you intend to apply any of our information in any way to your business operations.

This course is sold for entertainment purposes only, and the author, publishers and/or distributors are not responsible for any actions taken as a result of reading this course.

Terms of Use

You are given a non-transferable, "personal use" license to this book. You cannot distribute it or share it with other individuals.

Also, there are no resale rights or private label rights granted when purchasing this book. In other words, it's for your own personal use only.

Trademarks

Any and all trademarks, either written or shown in pictures, are the property of the respective trademark owners.

How to Become a Highly Paid Internet Joint Venture Broker

Table of Contents

Welcome..11
Exactly What Is Joint Venture Broking ?..........................13
    Here's a very simple example of a successful joint
    venture..13
    Other Names For Internet Joint Ventures....................14
  Why Would Companies Want To Get Involved In Your Joint
  Ventures?..15
  Five Good Reasons to Become a JV Broker Now.............16
    And Why This is a Great Time To Get Started…...........17
Joint Ventures' Biggest Secret Revealed..........................19
  Why Joint Venture Marketing May Just Be The Most
  Powerful Marketing Method Ever.....................................20
    Customer Relationships: The Secret Key!....................22
  Endorser, Endorsee And Broker ….How They All Work
  Together To Earn £££'s...24
    The Endorser..24
    The Endorsee..25
    The JV Broker...25
  But Selling is Still The Name of The Game.......................26
    An Example of Joint Ventures in Action......................28
    Summary...29
How And Where to Find JV Partners..................................31
  Who Makes A Good JV Partner?..31
  Three Great Joint Venture Ideas.......................................33
  Techniques For Finding All The Opportunities You Will
  Ever Need...34
    Internet Searches...34
    Using The Google Toolbar...36
    Using The Alexa Toolbar...37
    Using Networking..37
    Monitoring Advertisements...38
    Matching Competitors...39

Using Business Directories...39
Using Business to Business Mailing Lists.....................39
Using Web, Newsletter And E-Zine Directories...........40
Joining And Using Forums And Discussion Groups......41
Secret Sources of Internet Joint Venture Opportunities......43
Summary...44
Putting The Deal Together..47
Checking Out Your Prospective Partners......................47
JV Dealmaking Strategy...48
Sealing The Deal Made Simpler....................................49
Always Use The Right Approach..................................49
Contact The Right Person...50
Pitching Your Proposition...50
17 Powerful Sales Arguments To Use...........................51
More Powerful Sales Strategies....................................54
Four P's That Mean Profit..56
Summary...57
Joint Venture Agreements Revealed....................................59
The Basis of a Good Contract: Win-Win!.......................59
Tips And Pointers For Legal Agreements.....................62
The Financial Aspects of a JV Deal..............................64
Limited or Lifetime Commissions?...............................66
Summary...67
Joint Venture Marketing Techniques...................................69
Endorsement Marketing: Secrets Revealed.....................70
Indirect...71
Direct...72
Great Endorsements .... And How To Prepare Them.........73
More Types of Endorsement..74
Free Information/Resource Endorsement......................74
Product Endorsement..76
Endorsement Mediums...77
E-Zine Promotions And JV's...79
The Importance of Tracking Orders...............................81
Boosting Your IJV With OFFLINE Joint Ventures...........82
Top JV Marketing Blunders to Avoid.............................84
More Marketing Options For JV's...................................88
Sample Letters...91
Examples of Joint Venture Marketing Partnerships.......97

Profile of a JV in Action..99
50 Benefits of Joint Ventures And Joint Venture
Marketing..101
Useful Websites..105
7 Secrets of Web Wealth...109
    The Most Important Web Wealth Secret...........................111
    Secret #1 What Product to Sell...114
        Secret #2 What Should Your Web Site Look Like?......117
        Secret #3 Who Should Design Your Web Site?...........119
        Secret #4 How Many Products Should You Sell?........122
        Secret #5 Why Do People Use The Internet?...............122
        Secret # 6 The Landing Page and Credibility...............124
        Secret # 7 Driving Traffic to Your Site..........................128
    Questions..133

Welcome

Publisher's note: *This book is written by a UK author (spelling has been changed for US English) and as such uses Pounds, £, as the currency unit throughout but as this business is online it can be pursued pretty much by **any one anywhere in the world**. If you are in the US, simply substitute, in your mind, Pounds with Dollars, $, as you read. If you want to convert the example numbers, you can either check the current exchange rate or simply use £1 = $1.60 as a rough rule of thumb. This can be done for just about any currency anywhere in the world.*

As you probably know, there are dozens, maybe hundreds of ways to make money on the Internet. Some big – some small – some simple – and some more complex. But this is one I like to think of as a '*nothing business*'!

Why do I say that? Well, it is quite literally a business you can start with *nothing*:

…. You don't need any capital.

…. You don't need an office, shop or warehouse.

…. You don't need any experience.

…. You don't need to know anything much about the Internet.

…. You don't need to know anything much about marketing.

…. And most interesting of all you don't even need a product to sell!

But that doesn't mean it is not very profitable and worthwhile. Because although you can start with nothing but a desire to succeed, you can use your own ingenuity and effort – and the information you will read in this manual – and turn it into what I feel is one of the most lucrative and profitable opportunities in the history of the Internet so far.

Something for nothing often turns out to be nothing much worth having. But I think that, in this case, you will be as excited as I am at the potential that Internet Joint Venture Broking offers. Please read on now and find out exactly how!

Best Wishes

Paul Marlow

Exactly What Is Joint Venture Broking ?

(And Why You Should Get Involved Now!)

Joint ventures (JVs) are perhaps the most exciting thing to happen in the Internet business world – and in the world of making money – for many, many years. But they are not especially complicated. And, really, they are not even that new. In fact they are tried, tested and proven.

At its simplest, a joint venture is just an arrangement where two people or companies put their separate skills and resources into achieving something …. something that is much more powerful and profitable than the two parts could achieve individually.

Here's a very simple example of a successful joint venture

An author writes a book. A publisher publishes and sells it. They both make money from producing a product that people want to buy but the *joint venture* is really the key to it all. The writer couldn't publish, distribute and sell the book without the expertise of the publisher. And the publisher wouldn't have a product to sell without the author.

Joint ventures are long established and proven in the world of ordinary, 'offline' business …. where they can produce excellent results for both parties. But when you add the Internet into the equation they offer more than just excellent results …. they can produce fantastic, incredible, record-breaking results. (And that's an understatement in many cases!)

But like anything else there can be a bit of a snag with that type of joint venture. You see, in the ordinary world joint ventures normally happen between two or more established, up-and-running companies. Normally big companies. For example, airlines often compete in joint ventures to generate traffic for each other's routes. That's all very well if you're a big company with a lot of clout. But it's very difficult if you're a newcomer or small entrepreneur. Who could possibly want to joint venture with you? What have *you* got to offer? Probably not much.

That's where the Internet shows its incredible potential and makes big business available to the new or small entrepreneur once again. Because when you involve the Internet you don't need to be a British Airways or a Ford to cash in on joint ventures. You can do it all as a *broker*, starting with nothing …. simply bringing the parties together and setting up the deal. And of course claiming an excellent commission for your efforts.

In this manual we are going to explain how *Internet joint venture broking* works, and exactly how you can become an Internet joint venture broker, and exploit this quite awesome opportunity, yourself.

Note that joint ventures aren't the same as affiliate marketing. Anyone can sign up as an affiliate to a website and the rewards on offer are usually modest. Joint ventures are individually negotiated, and the potential returns are substantially higher.

Other Names For Internet Joint Ventures

When you're using the Internet, looking for information or making contacts, you might find other terms being used for joint venture marketing. All of the following terms can be found, and they mean more or less the same thing:

- Barter marketing.
- Collaborative marketing.

- Cross promotion marketing.

- Endorsement marketing.

- Fusion marketing.

- Internet network marketing.

- Reciprocal marketing.

Why Would Companies Want To Get Involved In Your Joint Ventures?

You might wonder why companies would want to get involved in Internet joint ventures with you, especially if they are already successfully established doing business on the Internet. There are many good reasons:

- All successful businesses eventually run into the same problem. After a while, they run out of products to sell, new markets to sell to, or both.

- They don't need much, or any, extra cash to enter into an Internet joint venture.

- The overheads for most Internet joint ventures are very low. So any extra sales are mostly profit.

- It can be quite difficult for one company to approach another company and propose a joint venture. Often they don't know how, don't know who, or don't want to be rejected.

That's why there are lots of opportunities for you – as a *broker* – to bring the parties together. You find a product that needs more customers, a company with customers who are eager to buy, bring them together and share in the extra profits.

Very quickly, with just a few joint venture agreements, you can go from 'no business' to 'big business' with little investment and little risk. It really can be a win-win situation for everybody involved.

Key Terms You Need To Remember

To avoid unnecessary repetition, I will use the following abbreviations throughout this book:

JV   : Joint Venture

IJV   : Internet Joint Venture

IJVM : Internet Joint Venture Marketing

IJVB   : Internet Joint Venture Broker (or Broking)

Five Good Reasons to Become a JV Broker Now

- You don't need to set up a business as such. You don't need a warehouse, or even an office – nor spend much time selling, dealing with customers, shipping orders etc. Your partners do all the 'work stuff' while you just set things up.

- You don't need to create and manufacture products, build any websites or do anything technical. (You'll have your choice of profiting from selling virtually any product or service in the world.)

- You don't need to spend lots of time and money building your own customer list. (You're going to tap straight into leads that'll make you tens or even hundreds of thousands of pounds …. so that means you can start making money right away.)

- You don't need to have a lot of contacts you've known for years. (You can actually be allowed to 'borrow' the name of almost any expert in any field and reap the benefits of being well-known …. even if you're 'unknown' right now!)

- You can get started in this business for next to nothing. What other kind of real business that leads to a good full time income from home costs less than that to get started?

And Why This is a Great Time To Get Started...

- Hardly anybody knows about this yet. It's becoming very popular in the USA, but hardly anyone in the UK even knows about it. There are still hundreds of thousands of opportunities yet to be exploited in every country.

- It's a global business. You aren't restricted to doing deals just in your own town. You can JV nationwide – and even worldwide.

- It's a risky time to be a manufacturer/producer/developer of anything – and often involves a huge outlay for small profits. But as an IJVB you don't have to invest anything, and you can't lose.

- You can be pulling in large profits in as little as 30 days time …. no waiting.

- It's the first skill anyone needs to learn for becoming successful in any business. (If you can't make money doing this you probably won't make money from any other business!)

- All the strategies, tactics and sales methods you need have already been developed by other successful operators. You don't need to spend years developing methods of your own. You just do what other successful JVB's have already done.

  (But their methods aren't patented or copyrighted, so you're free to do exactly the same.)

Joint Ventures' Biggest Secret Revealed

Don't Sell.... Endorse!

Although joint ventures are very easy to set up they are so effective due to many reasons – reasons that are connected with both complex marketing theory and even psychology. An understanding of these reasons will help you appreciate the very special ingredients that go towards making JV's so exciting.

Think about something for a minute. Let's say you are in business yourself. Someone, somewhere is able to wave a magic wand and give you just one of the following. Which would you prefer?

1. A free full-page advertisement in a publication with 150,000 subscribers?
2. A mailing list of those 150,000 subscribers, all ready to send your ad. out to, with the postage all paid for you?
3. To know somebody who knows those 150,000 people, and who has already done business with them and who is willing to recommend your product to their customers?

While both options 1 and 2 are very appealing there's no doubt that option 3 – the ready made relationship with those 150,000 subscribers through a friend-of-a-friend or whatever – is the one which is sure to be the most lucrative and profitable. (And, by the way, the easiest to do!)

What you should appreciate right now is that by following the principles of IJVB you *do* have a ready made relationship with those 150,000 business prospects (and in fact many, many more) and the ability to quickly and easily take advantage of them (in the nicest possible way of course).

We're not talking about placing ads. or sending direct mail here. We're talking about Internet joint venture endorsement marketing. Something that is even simpler and cheaper than the best offline direct marketing campaign. And something you can get started in without any experience or knowledge of traditional marketing at all!

Why Joint Venture Marketing May Just Be The Most Powerful Marketing Method Ever

Internet Joint Venture Marketing (IJVM) just may be the most powerful marketing method ever known! But why?

Its formidable strength is in making use of a powerful but often underutilized (or even unused) asset. By asset we are not talking about a machine, a truck or even a factory but the *company's customer database*.

Most businesses – assuming they are well run – should maintain a list of the people who have bought from them. This is particularly so in the case of companies involved in Internet commerce. This list could also be of enquirers …. those individuals who have expressed some interest in the company's products and/or services in the past. This makes them stand out from someone who has never contacted the company before. These people have in effect put up their hands and said *'I am willing to buy ???? (whatever it is) from you'* …. even though, perhaps, they have not actually bought.

Many businesses do not realize the value of this information. It is a golden rule in marketing that once a prospect becomes a customer they should be considered a potential customer for life. The same applies to enquirers. They can sell to those customers over and over again, for an indefinite period of time, because they have already established *trust*. (This is assuming that they sell good products and provide good service of course.) It is amazing, however, how many companies simply do not make use of the resource.

This customer relationship is a key element in Internet joint venture marketing. IJVM involves the recommendation or endorsement of one company or their product to the customer list of another company. You are the broker that puts the two elements together.

This endorsement contains two key aspects:

1. The existing relationship between the list owner and their previous customers/prospects.

2. The weight that a recommendation from someone you already know carries.

In simple terms the list owner is recommending the new product/product owner to their list. That's straightforward enough. But the established relationship is what turns a small response into a potentially massive response. And the involvement of the Internet in the whole process is what makes it cost effective and incredibly profitable.

The reason for the much higher sales percentage is based on the fact that these lists are what are known as 'hot lists'. What that means is that the list owner has already

established a relationship with the people on their mailing list. They trust the list owner. In contrast, you could have a 'cold' list. This is one that has never heard of the person mailing to the list. Most likely that person rented a list of names from a list broker and is just mailing blindly to a list that neither knows nor necessarily trusts them.

But can this sort of endorsement really make that much of a difference?

Experience proves that it can result in a truly massive difference! (And even better in money terms!)

Consider this example:

You rent a mailing list of 1,000 names and send them a sales letter selling a product for £40 and you receive a 2% response. That is 20 sales worth £800. That is the industry average for returns on cold lists.

Next, you enter into a JV with the person who owns that same list, has a relationship with those people and who endorses the product or service in question to the list by saying: "Buy this! You'll love it!" This time you receive 240 sales producing £9,600. That is a 24% return! Even if your JV partner receives 50% of the money, you're still far better off.

Can this happen? The answer is YES. (Although of course it depends on the list, the owner, the sales literature, product/service and how targeted a market the prospects were.)

Can you see the difference between what is known as an endorsed mailing and a cold mailing? This is extremely powerful stuff. You are leveraging the power of the list owner's relationship with their mailing list to bring in vastly increased sales. Even more important, the list members who buy from the list become customers of the second company. They have every right to add them to their own very powerful list and so on and so forth. This is a way to build powerful customer lists and endorsement sales very, very quickly.

This is an example from the world of traditional offline direct marketing of course – using direct mail sent through the post. The concept works much the same way on the Internet on a brokered basis – except it's easier and cheaper to do. You don't need to order any printing, or spend a fortune on postage! You don't even need a business or product of your own!

Customer Relationships: The Secret Key!

Customer relationships are very much the secret key that unlocks the phenomenal power of joint venture marketing.

The most important asset of any business is its customer relations. So much so that it's worth a business focusing most if not all of their business growth efforts on. In fact, most good businesspeople spend more money on building relationships with their customers than almost anything else. (And, best of all, all the effort they spend building customer relations can benefit you!

Here's a simple example of customer relations:

You get a 'courtesy call' from a company you have bought something from in the past – perhaps your bank or a car company. These people are building customer relations. The same applies if you get a newsletter or you're offered an e-mail bulletin or e-zine. They might be trying to sell you something, but the primary purpose is customer relations.

As you know, good businesses should maintain lists of their best prospects and customers. Often, they use these lists to send helpful information to them, in accordance with their efforts to build positive relationships with their prospects and customers. Why? Because relationships make up the greatest factor in sales.

It's very easy for one business to cash in on other businesses' relations with their customers to sell their products. You can do this as the owner of another business or, as in this case, as a broker. Here's how: Find business owners who cultivate the best relationships with their customers. (Any business that sends regular communications to their customers, prospects, distributors, or subscribers is very often outstanding in this regard, both online and offline.) Now use that company's relationship with their customers to sell another company's products.

All you have to do is ask those business owners to introduce another product or service to their audience. When they do this, in addition to offering that person a nice piece of every sale made from the endorsement, you'll rarely get rejected because the first company has already broken the ice and established the trust.

Do you see the super selling power in this?

Again, looked at from the point of view of if you were to buy or trade the customer list and mail your own letter, how much of a response would you get in comparison? If you do it using the conventional medium of 'snail mail' you'll probably get a 'reasonable' response. If you do it by bulk e-mail (which is prone to be regarded as spam) you might get *none*. But when you have that list owner endorse your offer to their customers you'll get many, many more times the response with the endorsement compared to a cold mailing!

Endorser, Endorsee And Broker ....How They All Work Together To Earn £££'s

Next let's break down the roles of each party involved in an IJV and see how they all fit together:

The Endorser

This is the list owner. You may wonder why a list owner would want to give a powerful endorsement for someone else to their customer list. However, it is simple and happens all the time:

- **To make money**: When one company endorses someone else's product to their list, they do so for a percentage of the profits. This can be quite a substantial percentage. Their outlay is low (almost non-existent in many cases) and whatever they do make is largely profit.

- **To enhance their image**: It is extremely time consuming to constantly create new products. So, instead of creating their own products the endorser can find other entrepreneurs offering high quality products that they like and set up a deal, through a broker. Normally, when the endorser recommends other useful, helpful, high quality products to their audience it can only help sales of their own product.

- **To test the responsiveness** of their list and maintain it: This is a good chance to see what their customers want to buy. If they buy the product that is endorsed, that is a good indication of what they will buy in the future.

The Endorsee

This is the person gaining an introduction to the list by having the list owner endorse their product or service. You may be wondering why this person would ever want to give up a significant percentage of their profits (which they often do) simply to be introduced to a list. Here's why:

- The endorsee has now gained new customers without spending advertising pounds. Even if they don't make much money on the first sale they could make thousands on and on into the future. The lifetime value of a customer far outweighs the cost of getting that new customer.

- The endorsee can make more profits with a JV than they ever could mailing to a cold list.

- They can 'piggyback' off the credibility of the list owner. This is especially valuable if they are a new or little-known company.

While some JV deals involve just an endorser and an endorsee there is potentially one other person in this deal …. and this could very well be you!

The JV Broker

This is a person (you?) who brings these two parties together and takes a percentage of the profits …. created out of nothing more than a list and a good idea.

You might wonder, why is there a need for brokers to do this?

The answer is that you can make potentially good profits simply for bringing a product and a list (essentially a supply and a demand) together. But in most cases the other parties often do not have any idea what kind of profits they are sitting on. And even if they do, have absolutely no idea how to go about setting it all up. Often they are just too busy doing the same old, same old.

As a JV broker you arrange the deal and educate the prospects in how this works and all you ask for is a share of the profits. You do not charge anything upfront for doing all this, but claim a commission. This makes your offer irresistible to prospective endorsers and endorsees, so it can be very easy to sign people up.

If you happen to have a product and mailing list up and running then you can operate joint ventures very successfully by becoming either an endorser or endorsee (or both). However, if you don't you can get involved in this lucrative opportunity, simply by becoming a broker. And, as I said in the introduction, you don't need a business, product, nor very much money to do so. This manual will show you exactly how.

But Selling is Still The Name of The Game

Many businesses forget that the purpose of all marketing is to make sales. It is not just about relationships, or image. At the end of the day the success of all advertising is solely measured by the amount of money you take versus the amount of money you spend. The best form of marketing you could ever hope to find is one that minimizes the outlay while maximizing the income you make.

Internet joint venture marketing scores very highly in this regard. Here are some of the reasons why:

1. It utilizes the special relationship between a company and their satisfied customers – people who have bought already and in doing so shown that they are almost certainly willing to buy again – in fact they probably *want* to buy again.

2. You (or the endorsee) only pay out on results. You don't pay for general effect and you don't get general effect …. you get sales.

Everyone earns based on results.

3. There are very few costs involved. You don't buy a mailing list, and if your endorsement is made using electronic methods, you don't have any printing or shipping costs either. Furthermore, few steps are involved in making the sale. Because of the nature of an endorsement, sales are usually made in one step.

4. It's an extremely targeted form of marketing. Endorsements are made between two similar businesses. In as much as the customers receiving the endorsement are customers of a similar business, or the prospects are the prospects of a similar business, or the subscribers are interested in your field, it can be presumed each person approached is interested in your offer.

5. The endorsement is made by a third party. People respect 'independent' endorsements far more than self-selling attempts. (Even if that company were to introduce their products to their audience they might not get as high a response as if they were to make a good endorsement of someone else's product of equal value.) Thus, joint venture deals are beneficial whether you make or receive the endorsement.

6. The endorsee can get potentially life-long customers out of these deals. You don't just make money from each customer's initial order, but from all the orders thereafter. Accordingly, it is often profitable to give the endorser most of the profits made on the order resulting from the endorsement, and simply benefit from each of the customer's future orders. The endorsee gets very 'upsellable' customers – the endorser just upsold the customer onto their products – so they can expect to make more money on the back end sales to that customer.

7. There has been a boom in recent years of small businesses working in unique niches.

With this, it is easy to set up joint ventures – most small businesses are very open to these arrangements. (This isn't to say that you can't broker JV deals with big, multinational companies …. because you can!)

8. Joint ventures can be carried out on the Internet via websites and e-mail or e-zine, and also by phone, fax, in a newsletter, seminar, conference call, in store, as a self-mailing, or as an insert etc.. Whatever is most appropriate to the product in question. Endorsements can be made at the point of purchase, after the purchase, to dormant customers, and even to prospects who have not yet ordered. In short it is an incredibly flexible way of selling.

An Example of Joint Ventures in Action

In one case we heard of an author selling a course for £197, including books and tapes, on finance and investment, who was getting about a 1.3% response from direct mailings to 'hot' customer lists. That's okay. But after the costs of buying the lists, the cost of their direct mail package, and the cost of sending the package out, he would get about a 110% return on his investment …. That's acceptable, but nothing spectacular. He then found out about joint venture marketing and set up an arrangement to market his course to a financial newsletter publisher at no cost.

After a little persuasion the newsletter publisher agreed to interview this author and endorse his course in his newsletter of over 11,200 subscribers. As a result of the endorsement, 948 people ordered within ten days of the newsletter being sent out... that's £186,756 in revenue! From each package, the original publisher received £100. That left the author about £75,840 in profits and 948 customers on their own mailing list to sell more products to. He then arranged several more endorsements where he only paid for the production of the endorsement and the return on his investment shot up from 110% to over 530%! When you take into account the back end, his investment return was actually much higher as he then successfully endorsed several products to his customers.

Why does the response rate jump so much just because of the endorsement of the list owner? It seems complex but really is simple. The customers or subscribers have dealt with Company

'X' for some time now. They have started to trust them. The recommendation is taken highly by them. The most powerful form of marketing is word of mouth and this is where word of mouth can come into play and practically guarantee the success of both companies involved.

This is only one example of how a joint venture can work. There are really infinite possibilities which can be brought into the equation to make them more successful and risk free.

Summary

If you were to think of every business technique that you have ever learned this one probably has the potential to produce more profits than anything else. And it is the easiest and quickest way to produce a positive cash flow in just about *any* business.

It is really that powerful!

It can be used to make an almost instant success of practically any business, especially when you have all of the tools available to you online. Just about any business can be involved, both new and old, products or services. It doesn't matter. What does matter is the fact that a properly set up JV can be a win-win proposition for absolutely everyone involved.

Before I go any further, let me stop for a moment and make sure you understand exactly what IJVM is all about. Although it sounds like a difficult idea at first to learn, the whole premise behind it is extremely simple. Joint Venturing is taking the unused assets in a business (i.e. essentially customers but also advertising, products, services, knowledge, skills, etc.) and leveraging them with another company with a product to sell to produce almost immediate profits for the both of them …. to say nothing of the person who brokers the deal.

Everyone wins in this deal. Once you understand just how simple it is to take advantage of joint ventures, you will wonder how you could have ever done business without this no-risk marketing strategy!

Apply the following questions to almost any business and you will see that almost any could be involved:

- What does the business do?
- What do they specialize in?
- Who are their customers?
- What *else* would their customers like (or need) to purchase or use?

Many times other business owners never ask themselves these crucial questions and so don't realize what a gold mine they are sitting on. By asking those questions <u>for them</u> you can earn yourself a fortune.

Key Terms You Need To Remember

Endorser …. or Host: The party who introduces an offer or product/service to their existing customer group. This is the 'list owner'.

Endorsee …. or Beneficiary: The party who has a product/service to sell, and wishes it to be introduced to another company's customers.

The Broker: The party who brings the other two parties together to create a profitable deal …. YOU!

How And Where to Find JV Partners

Now that you have a good understanding of what IJVM is about you are ready to get started actually setting up JV deals. The first step is to look for JV partners, both endorsers and endorsees, whom you can link together.

Who Makes A Good JV Partner?

Thousands, if not tens of thousands of companies in the UK alone (and millions worldwide) are potential partners for your JV deals. But to maximize your chances of success you need to set some basic minimums. You won't have all of this information to hand at the 'looking' stage, but try and use it to filter out those partners which are unsuitable.

The potential *endorser* (list owner) should:

- Be well known in the industry/subject in question. Their recommendation will go a very long way and their word is often gold to their customers and contacts.

- Possess a *large* existing customer list. This is SO important. You can make money from a list of 100 names – but the more names the more you stand to make from much the same work. Ideally the list should not be smaller than 1,000 names and they should be 40% (ie. 400) paying customers compared to enquirers. Ideally they should all be paying customers.

- Be able to handle the marketing (on the Internet, bulk e-mailing etc.) for the endorsee. Since the endorser is the one who has the relationship with their list they will have a better idea of what techniques will generate the greatest response from their customers.

This also applies to creating or writing the literature itself. You, or the endorsee, can help or advise. But at the end of the day take the advice of the people who know their customers best.

The potential *endorsee* should:

- Have a good quality product/service that the endorser has no problems putting their valuable reputation behind. You are asking them to risk their credibility on this product or service. It had better be good! Other than that there are virtually no limits on what products and services you can JV with.

- Be able to handle fulfillment of the product …. unless this is something that the endorser particularly wants to handle.

- Be able to handle all the administration, payments etc. to the endorser so they have nothing else to do other than send out the endorsement. (In some cases it can be better if the endorser handles the payment, sends the endorsee their cut and then the endorsee takes care of fulfillment. This can be a suitable option if the endorsee is a very new company without a proven history, or if they are abroad etc. it will avoid potential problems and may also look better to the end customer.)

- Be willing for the endorser to take the lead with marketing – for the reasons mentioned above. They might know their product well, but it is <u>customer</u> knowledge rather than <u>product</u> knowledge that really matters here.

Good Tip: Look for a niche, or a few niches. That is one specific product or a number of very closely related products. Once you understand one niche it is relatively easy to duplicate the same tactics and strategies in as many other niches as you want!

Three Great Joint Venture Ideas

JV With Competitors: Team up several weaker competitors in a JV to compete with their stronger rivals. Helps them sell more and cut costs.

JV With Publishers: Set up deals where Internet publishers (e-zines and e-books etc.) JV with businesses selling other products and services.

JV With Visitors: Set up deals where visitors to your endorsers' and endorsees' sites are allowed to use material and sell products using an affiliate scheme – so your partners' site's customers actually become global salespeople for the site. This is a form of what is known as *viral marketing.*

Three Simple Steps to Identify Thousands of JV Ideas

Here is one simple technique for you to find joint ventures on your own on the Internet. The Internet is not only a great way to set up a JV, but a great way to identify them too. Just follow these three simple steps:

Step One: Decide/research what your product area should be. For example: Sports, motoring, fashion, finance, health, software, consultancy, entertainment etc. At this stage just try your own ideas and thoughts since, as a broker, you aren't committed to any one product. Don't just restrict yourself to one idea, try lots. And don't be afraid to play around with unusual ideas at this stage!

Step Two: Go to one of the major search engines – any one – and search for keywords which relate to your targeted product area.

Step Three: Browse the results and chose those specific products which seem to be popular and successful right now. You are especially looking for websites selling them which seem to have carved out a niche in the market, and which offer good quality and good service.

In many cases you might even consider buying/using the products/services yourself first, as a customer, to get a really good idea as to whether they will make good JV products.

Remember that you don't need to get too involved with what the product is, how it works, is designed and made etc. One of the great things about IJVM is that you don't need to have a product of your own, or much product knowledge, to get started!

Techniques For Finding All The Opportunities You Will Ever Need

One of the most important aspects of broking JV deals is to find the best possible partners to participate in them – whether as endorsers or endorsees – from amongst the many hundreds or many thousands of companies available. The more effort you put into this research and development stage the more successful you are likely to be.

The best advice at this stage is to cast your net as widely as possible, and list as many companies as you possibly can. Don't restrict yourself to too narrow a search. Unsuitable partners can be 'weeded out' at a later stage but, generally, the more prospects you have the better. Even if a prospect turns out to be unsuitable for one deal they could prove ideal for another.

However, at least in the early days, a handful of suitable partners is better than hundreds. By all means consider a large number of prospective partners but it is better to actually create deals with only a select few of them initially.

All these methods are particularly suitable for finding partners for Internet JV's. They include both conventional offline methods and other methods that are specifically for locating businesses who are involved actively in e-commerce. Bear in mind that the methods may also vary depending on what you want to sell.

Internet Searches

As I have already said, by doing Internet searches with

appropriate keywords and phrases, you can find many excellent joint venture leads. Just type the product you are interested in into your search engine, and variations of it, to see what comes up.

This works because websites who are highly ranked by the search engines are very often also the biggest and most popular companies for that product. However, in practice these websites are actually only the most linked-to. They may be but are not necessarily the biggest/best known in that particular business. Don't be afraid to move further down the search engine rankings, since these companies may have perfectly good products. They are less likely to have JV arrangements anyway (participating in JV's may enhance their position in the rankings too) and, being smaller, may be more interested and easier to deal with.

Don't concentrate on just the sponsored or paid-for listings. This can distort the 'popularity' stakes. And don't just restrict yourself to Google. Other search engines can produce lesser-known and more interesting contacts.

Search for all the key words associated with the product you are interested in. Also search for plurals and words similar to or variations on those key words – a thesaurus is handy here. Sometimes, you can produce interesting contacts by searching for misspelled words, and foreign words or versions of the word. For example, if you are looking for car-related products try 'car', 'cars', 'motors', 'motoring', 'automobile' (the usual American word for car).

You'll need to set some kind of limit to make this task manageable. Initially visit the first ten sites that come up. Then contact the owners to find out if they are interested in working a JV with you – and make sure they are not selling a product that is competing with anything else you are handling. Subsequently you can move on to the next ten and so on, up to about a maximum of 250 listings.

Once you start this process you will find that it can prove quite time consuming. Ideally you want to make it as painless as possible. There are a number of ways to do this.

Try using an *automated search software program* – see my 'Useful Websites' section for contacts. These systems will visit the other search engines for you and give you the most relevant sites that come up on all of them, under your chosen keyword. The basic service is often free and you can purchase upgrades which allow more accurate searching.

Here are a couple more highly recommended techniques:

Using The Google Toolbar

The Google Toolbar is a free browser plug-in that you download to your computer and which integrates with Internet Explorer (IE5 or higher). Visit www.toolbar.google.com for details. As you surf from site to site using the toolbar it will provide you with background information about the site. (Google Toolbar has other features which you might find useful, although they are not strictly relevant to this task.)

One thing that Google Toolbar tells you is a website's page rank or PR. This is a measure of how important Google think the site is, on a scale of 1-10. Google measure a site's importance by how many links it has. Since links usually mean a lot of traffic – and you primarily want sites with a lot of traffic – this is a good way to find them.

Another good feature of the Google Toolbar is that it allows you to see who is linking to a particular site. Look for the blue circle with the letter 'I'. Clicking on this will provide information on those links. Not only can this indicate good traffic, but can also offer up other opportunities for JV's.

An alternative way to benefit from this information is to visit a close competitor's site. You can see who *their* biggest links are to, and consider them as JV contacts for the initial site you were interested in.

Using The Alexa Toolbar

The Alexa Toolbar which you can obtain from www.alexa.com offers all kinds of information about the site you are visiting including estimated traffic statistics, information on the website owner, comments others have made about the site and much other useful information which isn't found on Google.

It is probably worth having both Google and Alexa. However, bear in mind that the Alexa information can be slightly biased. The information provided is largely obtained from those who have the Alexa toolbar installed. So, if not many web surfers in your chosen product area use Alexa you can get distorted results.

One very handy feature that Alexa does have is 'WayBack'. This provides information on how long the site has been established, and how traffic has changed over time. It enables you to check whether a site has always been popular – or just become popular (which may not necessarily last).

Other Toolbars/Software: Although the Google and Alexa toolbars are regarded as market leaders they are not necessarily the only tools you can use for this job. There are other toolbars and software on offer and regularly being created, some of which are free and others charged for. If you have or find a favorite tool then by all means use it. Just bear in mind that most of these tools and software have some slight glitches or drawbacks, so they are only an aid to the procedure and the information they reveal shouldn't be regarded as definitive.

Finally, once you find these sites you will need to contact the owner. If the owner is not stated on the website then you can perform a 'whois' search using one of the website research services (see 'Useful Websites') to reveal who actually owns and operates the site.

Using Networking

This is a mainly offline way of developing contacts for online

JV's.

Networking associates are people you come into contact with in the course of your normal business, or even social life. They might be colleagues, customers, suppliers, friends, casual acquaintances etc. In other words, you don't automatically think of them as JV partners – but they could be.

Try to build and stay in contact with a group of network associates. One of the major factors in being able to succeed in Internet marketing is the ability to quickly capitalize on opportunities when they arise. Building a contact base of business associates will help you do this. Plus, it will bring about all kinds of strategic alliance opportunities. There is no better place to draw JV endorsement deals from than your own group of network associates.

Get your name out there and let people know that you are a potential player in e-commerce. Go to the forums and participate! Participate in mailing lists and let people see your signature file. Get your name known! It will make you more credible when you approach one of the 'big guns' and request a deal.

Monitoring Advertisements

As a general principle in marketing, when you see adverts. run over and over again in any kind of media, it tends to suggest that someone is being very successful with a product, service or program, ie. they will have a healthy existing customer list which you can tap into. These people are also very often savvy marketers too, so they can be excellent prospects for a JV.

Analyze advertisements of all kinds and watch for re-run advertisements. Respond to the ad. and do some research until you find the contact information for the person running the ad. (it may not be the same as for orders). At some stage, the advertiser could become the perfect endorser for a product, or even an endorsee.

Matching Competitors

Any companies who you might consider are direct competitors can very often be good joint venture partners – unless the products they sell might conflict badly. For example, Pepsi and Coke wouldn't make good joint venture partners. But any two publishers who sell complementary books might be good joint venture partners since they both sell to the same customers who are likely to buy both products, not 'either/or'.

If you have a competitor that sells products worth endorsing as well as products that would replace the products the other partner sells in most cases this could make a very good JV. You may be able to set restrictions as to any back end promotions if you fear that one competitor would steal the other's customers in a joint venture, through back end sales. In most cases they won't, because they will know (or soon realize) that they have more to gain from continuing JV deals than using it as a sneaky way of beating their competitors.

Using Business Directories

Any business directory is a straightforward, direct way for finding joint venture partners or associates. The 'Yellow Pages' is perhaps the most popular choice here, but there are lots of other smaller online and offline directories, including specialized industry-related directories. Try an Internet search and don't forget to check the paper directories in the business and commercial section of the library.

Often, the more directories a company appears in the more likely it is to be interested in new marketing opportunities, such as JV's.

Using Business to Business Mailing Lists

Just as consumer mailing lists are used in mail order for obtaining the addresses of people likely to buy a product, so business to business (B2B) mailing lists are lists of companies trading in a particular product or service. They are a good way of finding prospective partners with good offline products that might translate well to the Internet (ie. endorsees). They may also have customer lists which you can use, as endorsers.

B2B mailing lists can be rented from list brokers. Try an Internet search to provide useful contacts (also see 'Useful Websites'). Contact the people that sell lists you're interested in and ask for the data sheet. This should give you information as to exactly what products the company deals in and who the most important decision makers are.

Using Web, Newsletter And E-Zine Directories

The Internet now hosts a number of specialized online directories which, although most are not specifically devoted to JV's, are very good for finding contacts.

Website Directories : If you wish to set up JV's with other dedicated web marketers, web directories sorted by category are useful. There are some to try listed in our 'Useful Websites' section.

Newsletter Directories: Internet newsletter directories are widely regarded as an excellent resource for finding JV partners. Newsletter publishers tend to have great relationships with their customers. And the publishers that list themselves in these directories are usually very open to JV deals, if you approach them correctly. Plus, these publishers are usually in monthly contact with their audience, and the newsletter itself provides a platform for the joint venture whereby the endorsee doesn't even have to pay for printing or shipping in most cases. Furthermore, the endorsee can often be interviewed by these newsletter publishers and have their interview along with a plug for the product appear in the newsletter, which is a very effective way of selling it.

E-Zine Directories: If you want to run joint venture endorsements with e-zine publishers, e-zine directories are good places to find them. Some of the biggest e-zines have over 100,000 subscribers, and e-zine joint venture endorsements have been proven to be very profitable. In the USA, e-zines are already a very powerful media and heavily involved in JV marketing. They are still very much a developing media in the UK but bound to become more important.

There are a number of directories where you can find newsletters and e-zines listed and described. We have listed some of these in the 'Useful Websites' section at the end of the book. Another good way to find e-zines is to run an Internet search using the terms 'e-zine', 'e-zine directory' or 'newsletter' and your chosen subject. (This is also likely to identify the most current and popular e-zines.)

Remember that if you want to arrange a JV with a newsletter or e-zine publisher then you should be subscribed to their product anyway so you know what it's all about. Some of the directory websites have a facility to allow you to sign up for as many as you want instantly.

Good Tip: Most newsletters and e-zines feature content from *guest authors*. These authors will have a signature at the end of their article to identify themselves. These people often have considerable influence by virtue of the fact that their article was featured in someone else's publication. Often, guest authors also have their own e-zine. So, you should keep a file in which you keep track of guest authors and other people you may want to joint venture with. Consider joint venturing with these authors if they're running compatible operations.

Joining And Using Forums And Discussion Groups

Internet forums and discussion groups provide online communities of like-minded people which, although intended for information sharing and contact building, can also be a very good place to look for JV partners. This is because they are mainly used by people positively looking for/willing to give assistance – and you might also find other people actually looking for JV's there. Again, many of them are US-based, but they can be used by anyone from around the world.

Forums: To find a good selection of forums type 'forum' and your chosen subject, 'Internet marketing forum' or even 'JV forum' into your search engine and you should get a good selection of current, busy forums. You can also try a forum directory for contacts.

The important thing about using a forum is that you must be willing to participate. Offers won't just come to you if you don't. If you're unsure about doing this, offer some advice to another member first – before you ask for it.

Discussion Groups: Discussion groups related to your field are great places to make joint venture contacts. As you participate in discussion groups, you build relationships with key people with whom you'll easily be able to set up joint venture deals. Pay attention to people's signatures. When you see someone with a signature that would

indicate they're running an operation compatible with yours make a note of their website. Keep checking back with their websites periodically to see what opportunities are available.

You can find web discussion groups using most Internet search engines but

Yahoo! Message Boards (www.messages.yahoo.com) and Lycos Search Message Boards (www.lycos.com) are most suitable for this. Forums and discussion groups are also often listed in the same places as e-zines, so use the e-zine directories already suggested to find them.

Cross Promotion Forums: Many cross promotion 'meeting places' now exist on the Internet. Unlike ordinary forums these are used by people not just looking for/offering help but actually looking to set up various types of joint ventures, including reciprocal links, e-zine cross advertising, and joint venture endorsements. You can find cross promotion forums using an Internet search. Also see our 'Useful Websites' section.

Secret Sources of Internet Joint Venture Opportunities

- Successful businesses, either online or currently offline, that have thousands of existing satisfied customers but no back end products to sell them. Simply find more products to sell to them, and broker a deal between the supplier and the original company.

- A busy, well-used website that doesn't seem to be exploiting its massive traffic levels much – or at all. It might not even be selling any products at all. Simply identify products and services that visitors are likely to want or need. Then approach the site owner and offer to arrange a supply.

- A business which has an online presence – ie. a website – but which doesn't record and keep in regular contact with its customers. Contact the owner and suggest they set up a regular newsletter or e-zine, which they can then use to offer their customers useful endorsements and helpful products and services.

- A product that already sells well but which could sell so much better with other marketing, or when offered through other channels. Good example: Book publishers who only sell their books in paper versions. You could offer to help with turning the book into an e-book, then market the e-book to a suitable list from one of your other partners.

- Also, look for products which you believe could be great sellers but which the manufacturer or supplier doesn't yet have an affiliate program for. Offer to set up an affiliate program for them in return for a cut of the proceeds. Although affiliate programs aren't the same as joint ventures this is a great toe-in to a more lucrative deal in the future.

- eBay sellers – those with a lot of feedback, including Power Sellers. Don't forget that eBay is a major and growing center for traffic on the Internet and you don't have to sell a product yourself to tap into it. Instead, contact existing sellers who possess a good mailing list of existing customers and then look for other products which they could sell to it. Harnessing excellent back end sales from these lists can be as simple as preparing an e-mail for the existing seller to mail out.

Time Saving Tip

Once you have contact details for prospective partners you are going to want to contact them all. This could be a very tedious process if you have a lot of contacts. You need to contact them all individually so that it is more personalized. However, you should try to minimize the amount of time that you spend on administrative tasks so you can concentrate on marketing.

One time saving option is to use a specialized e-mail client program that will let you send out personalized e-mail to your list, for your initial approach, without sending each message individually. To make this effective, load contact details into the system when you are researching contacts rather than later. It is easier to delete the contacts you never use than to go back looking for the best ones later on.

Summary

Now that we are well on the way to JV profits, you might find this quick summary of the process helpful:

1. Understand how and why IJVM works.

2. Take a product idea.

3. Find potential partners.

4. Approach potential partners.

5. Set the ground rules for the JV.

6. Market and sell the product.

7. Collect the profits.

8. Use what you have learned to put together your next joint venture!

Putting The Deal Together

Now you have the contacts for prospective JV's. The next step is to put the deal together. Fortunately, creating even the most powerful JV's is essentially quite simple in that you can work through a systematic checklist for each one.

Checking Out Your Prospective Partners

Use all the resources we have already discussed to find businesses which meet the following requirements. Note: This is an 'ideal world' situation. In some cases you might overlook some of these requirements if the partners look favorable in other ways.

⁻ They have a strong relationship with their customers, who would serve as good prospects for more offers.

⁻ They periodically contact these people in an effort to build good will, and:

⁻ They (probably) have a large enough mailing list or database for a joint venture endorsement to be attractive to you.

⁻ Their product is good! Too many marketers whether JV or (most particularly) affiliates totally overlook the quality and desirability of the product – preferring to concentrate on only the bottom line profit. Ask yourself, how good is the product …. really? How does it compare to similar products on the market? What sort of service does the supplier provide? Would you buy the product yourself?

⁻ Go for a high-profit product, at least when you start out. In joint venture endorsement marketing it's easier to get 100 people to send you £300 than it is to get 1,000 people to send you £20.

⁻ Avoid products that are connected with too many affiliate programs. Ideally you make the endorsement before the product's life cycle burns out. Therefore, you have to watch carefully and catch it before it comes too big.

⁻ If the prospective partner (especially if they are a prospective endorser) already has an e-mail bulletin or e-zine then sign up to it *immediately*. This will give you a good idea as to whether they will be suitable, and will also help when it comes to creating marketing literature.

At this stage you will have some idea whether each prospect is likely to be an endorsee or an endorser. However, don't fix your ideas just yet. You may well find that the roles can be reversed or even combined.

Good Tip: Consider buying the product. This isn't just to test how good/bad it is. If you do this then, when you contact the prospective partner, you can claim that you are a customer …. or even a long-time user. Very often this can mean your proposal is considered more seriously. (And, if you buy the product anyway, then you might as well get it from someone with whom you can set up a JV partnership.)

JV Dealmaking Strategy

Before you set out you need to know what's important about the good JV deal and, most importantly, how to convey that importance to your prospective partners.

The secret in this regard is to aim to always work with companies that maintain excellent relations with, and frequently contact, their customers. (As a business owner involved in joint venture marketing you should, of course, also frequently contact your customers.) This will open the door for cross promotions as well as instant profit hosting opportunities without the need to spend time developing a good customer relationship.

The more attractive a company becomes as an endorser, the more attractive they become as an endorsee and vice versa. Very few direct marketing companies will (or should) refuse good cross endorsement opportunities if they are presented in the right way. Part of making yourself attractive for joint ventures is creating a strong competitive advantage – the best direct marketers always work with related businesses that have a strong competitive advantage.

IJVM should be approached from a scientific marketing standpoint. You should do careful market research to find all the best businesses that are attracting your type of prospects and customers. **Joint venture endorsements should be focused on results, not general effect.**

Lastly, it is often a good idea that JV's are tested in a small way before being rolled out fully. This is as much to reassure the endorser as the endorsee.

Sealing The Deal Made Simpler

Always Use The Right Approach

Build a list of potential partners using the methods we've already discussed and then set about contacting the owner of each business. It is normally best to do this by letter using conventional mail, telephone or even fax. Although this seems strange for a heavily Internet-dependent business it is best not to rely on e-mail alone to make the initial contact. Many people get a lot of junk mail and there's always the risk they will think your e-mail is spam – especially when your offer is so good it might seem too good to be true! You can use e-mail to agree the details later, one you've made the initial introduction.

However, if you have built a very large list of contacts (in some product areas there could be hundreds of prospective partners) it could take weeks just to contact each person by mail, fax or phone. So you could try e-mailing each of them an ice-breaking/teaser e-mail message on the basis that some are bound to respond and this will be enough to get things started with. Then, when you contact them using the other method they will already have an idea of what is on offer. However – *and this is very important* – if you don't get a response to an e-mail don't cross them off your contact list.

Contact The Right Person

Aim to contact the owner of the business concerned – or at least a director, senior manager or marketing manager (some companies now have an Internet marketing manager). Don't explain your proposition to a junior employee or a secretary who isn't in a position to make a decision like this.

Make sure you always personalize your communications. In some businesses you may need to deal with several people. As you build your list of contacts, put their contact information into an e-mail database program. Personalizing communications is one of the best ways of building a relationship and building a deal. If you are not sure who to contact initially – ask!

Pitching Your Proposition

Bear in mind that your sales pitch will be slightly different depending on whether the contact is a prospective endorser or endorsee. When contacting endorsees the message is very simple: Explain to the relevant contact that you represent a well respected marketer with thousands of subscribers …. and you're sure your endorsement can generate tens of thousands of pounds of extra business for them. Tell them that your joint venture won't actually cost them anything up front, since you 'only' take a commission based on results.

Your initial contact can say something like 'Hello Mr Smith, this is Adam Johnson. If I can show you how to make a large sum of money by tapping into a massive ready market for your product …. And it would cost you absolutely nothing …. And I would do all the work involved but have you get all the credit …. Would you be willing to share this new profit with me?'

When contacting endorsers the message is switched around to put the focus on the product: Explain to the relevant contact that you represent a well-respected product manufacturer .... and you're sure that their customers would find it interesting and valuable. Tell them that you're in a position to negotiate a special deal .... and a generous commission on sales.

For example: 'If I can show you a way to make thousands of pounds extra profit .... Using an underutilized resource in your company .... Without charging you a penny .... And benefiting your existing customers too .... Would you be interested?.'

Any businessman or woman with an ounce of enterprising spirit will (or should) find it hard to totally ignore such an offer.

In either case it doesn't matter if you are talking to an endorsee but don't yet have an endorser, or vice versa. If you're using the methods we've already discussed and doing enough research and contact-making it won't be long before you have enough to create a successful JV.

17 Powerful Sales Arguments To Use

Here are some more useful sales arguments to use when selling prospective partners the idea of entering into a JV with you (some for endorsers, some for endorsees, some for both):

- It's easy to set up.

- This is a very targeted form of marketing, so you capture a selective audience.

- You can increase your income potential and profit margins dramatically.

- Depending on the type of joint venture, it costs you almost nothing.

- People have a tendency to respond better to endorsements,

rather than buying a product outright.

- Build credibility from other successful marketers and establish new business relationships.

- You can endorse products on your website or newsletter and receive a percentage of the sale.

- When you do a joint venture on other business websites, you are gaining link popularity.

- We have customers who are good prospects for your business and/or we have a product which we believe will sell successfully to your customers. (There is no need to reveal that you are a broker rather than a principal at this stage.)

- We would like to form a strategic alliance with you, for mutual profit!

- We know you've spent a good deal of time, effort, and money building goodwill with your customers/developing and marketing your product. This will help you get the returns you deserve.

- This alliance will help you capitalize on this underutilized/unused asset. In other words, your goodwill among customers, in a way more effective than any other. Or gain more sales for your product with hardly any effort.

- We would like you to sample our product so you can decide for yourself. We think our product would benefit your customers. And, if you agree after sampling the product, I would like to make your customers a special offer if you would be willing to introduce it to them.

- This form of endorsement marketing is a very effective way to capitalize on the goodwill you have with your customers because when you endorse someone else's product to them, they're more responsive than when you try to sell your own products to them.

- Our product, combined with a special offer, will mean that your customers will be literally thankful that you offered them this opportunity. So, as well as the profits, this can only enhance your business!

- Better still, we would be happy to give you most of the profits from the deal!

- This proposition involves few additional costs and no additional risk.

Don't run through this list in a robotic fashion. Just use this as a guide to the points you need to cover. Modify what you say according to how the contact responds. If the person you contact seems even slightly interested then you can go into more details about what is actually involved, ie. it is an Internet joint venture, and you are the broker setting up the deal.

Important: When you approach prospective partners you'll need to be persistent – but also be courteous. Remember that these people normally have businesses that are up-and-running anyway. So they don't have to agree to your deal. Many of them will not really understand what it is all about or the benefits, until you get a chance to explain it to them. And if they do turn you down, either later on in the negotiations or even straight away, don't get annoyed or angry about it. Thank them for their time and move onto the next prospect – there's every chance they'll come back to you in future just once they realize what a great opportunity they've turned down.

Also Important: When working with endorsees always stress that the real money is in the back end sales. And since any people that buy their product based on your endorsement have been 'back ended' – they can be sure these are very back-endable customers. Therefore, they shouldn't worry too much about the profits on the initial sale, but should be very open about the sort of deal that they might agree to. Point out that most successful businesses earn many times the amount of money on back end sales than on front end sales.

Sample Sales Letters

At the end of this manual you will find some sample sales letters which are suitable for use when contacting prospects for JV's. These are suitable for use as letters, faxes or e-mails and you can modify them to suit your own purposes.

More Powerful Sales Strategies

By this point in the manual you should know just what a fantastic proposition an Internet JV will be. But you need to realize that your prospective partners may need more persuading. Perhaps they are still not clear what a JV involves – or it may be that they've had a bad experience with another venture before. So, in some cases, it might be necessary to use some special selling tactics to take the deal further.

Here are some of the methods you can use. These methods are especially relevant to attracting the endorser, ie. the party who will be promoting the product you have found to their customers.

- Make It Easy: Offer to provide or even write the endorsement and any other literature that's needed. Interviews often work well as an endorsement, so point out that you can arrange this as a 'no brainer' method of promotion.

- Make A Special Offer: In order to get many companies to endorse your product, you have to make them feel like they're doing something good for their customers. So make a special offer that they can pass on to their customers. That might be a 50% discount, 25% discount, special bonus offer, or whatever. This special offer will also help in writing the endorsement itself as the endorser can show their audience how they went out and arranged a special deal just for them.

Remember – you'll all probably be able to make a much better special offer than you think because the endorsement is costing next to nothing in terms of marketing outlay!

- Remove The Risk: It is very important to emphasize that a JV arrangement won't jeopardize the endorser's existing business. Make sure they understand that their customers can buy from both them and you – you won't be taking away any customers or any business.

- If they're still not entirely convinced about this tell them that, if they wish, they can test the endorsement on a portion of their customer group to see if they respond positively. If they do they can then roll out the endorsement to their entire customer file.

- Make it financially appealing. Give an example of figures that could result from the endorsement. Tell them that responses are frequently ten or more times higher when someone endorses a product to their customers rather than offers their own product.

- Try to give specific figures, to add realism. This can be tricky and may involve guesstimates at this stage, but it really adds impact. You could say, 'For example, if you have 8,000 customers or subscribers, and if 10% of them ordered, that would be 800 times £80 which is £64,000 gross. And after the costs, you would be entitled to 60% of the profits, which would be about £??.'.

Generally, you shouldn't discuss exact potential sales and commission figures until you feel sure that the other party is seriously interested in the JV. Then, when you say something like *'Does an extra £??? profit sound good to you?'* you can see what impact this will add to the negotiations.

Don't be afraid to give examples like this. It excites people – especially when you mention real money and they can visualize cashing the checks and spending the money!

Four P's That Mean Profit

When you are operating an Internet business – where everything is, or is supposed to be, on demand – it's easy to forget some of the *basic principles of good business*. But these basic principles can make the difference between making and breaking a deal. Applying the four P's to your negotiations, even if they are fired off in an e-mail, really can help you seal the deal.

Politeness: Your JV offer may be fantastic and unmissable but bear in mind that the best prospective JV partners are already successful in business and may already be well-regarded as leaders in their field. So they will always respond better to being treated politely and with respect …. even if they seem to be slightly arrogant about their success and don't treat you politely!

Already-successful people don't have to make a deal with you. So try to remain polite no matter how long the negotiations might last, or even if they are quite negative at first. Don't take the attitude that they 'must be mad' not to be interested, or are 'losers'.

Patience: So you've e-mailed off more detailed information about your JV, which the prospective partner asked for. But an hour later you haven't received a response! In these situations, don't entirely dismiss the contact. The fact that a partner is taking time to think

about your offer is normally a good sign not a bad sign, and they could come back to conclude a deal weeks or even months later. Keep the contact on the list unless you are absolutely, definitely sure they are not interested.

Persistence: If you get no response at all – but are fairly sure there is good potential here – don't give up. Some communications get overlooked (this is especially the case with e-mails). Successful people have lots of other things to do and even pursuing new opportunities can come well down a list of priorities beyond dealing with emergencies and current problems. Again, keep proposing your JV until you are absolutely, definitely sure they are not interested.

Persuasion: If you have used all the previous 'P's' and your JV's are obviously being considered but are you are still not making deals then you should ask yourself if you are being persuasive enough? The solution is to aim to be more persuasive – rather than trying to change the deal, ie. by offering better commissions. Go back through the list of powerful sales strategies and ask yourself if you are using them, and if you are really pushing the *endorser/endorsee benefits* in each case.

Summary

Even when you use all your techniques do not put all your efforts into too few prospective partners. And certainly don't focus all your attentions on one particular one, no matter how good they seem. There will always be some people who say no, no matter how good your proposition – so when everything else fails just tick them off your list (make a note to contact them again in future if you think it could be worthwhile) and start again with new prospective partners from the hundreds of thousands to choose from globally.

Joint Venture Agreements Revealed

Once you've reached agreeable terms with either an endorsee or an endorser (or both) it is time to make a more *formal agreement* to confirm the details of your arrangement and how it is going to operate.

This is almost certainly going to involve some sort of contract. However, big, wordy, formal contracts scare many people. Simple contracts are just as binding, easier to agree and less likely to lead to problems over the fine details. If you really need to, ask a lawyer to advise on your contracts. But a simple letter of agreement is very easy to create and use. Outline the terms of the deal, ie. what you agree to do, and what the other person agrees to do. Write down the commission terms and everything you have agreed on. Then have both parties sign the letter.

Sensible: Your agreement should be created with IJVM in mind. You may come across standard distributor, agency or affiliate contracts (including many which have been published on the Internet) but often these do not accurately reflect the nature of this arrangement.

The Basis of a Good Contract: Win-Win!

Successful business arrangements rarely revolve around pedantic contracts and finely-worded clauses. They usually come about as a result of deals where everybody gets what they want (and more) from the arrangement and it's stated in plain English.

One of the great things about IJV's is that everybody stands to make money – a lot of money – from the arrangement. Together with many other benefits including potential for future back end sales, generating powerful customer mailing lists, good publicity and enhanced credibility.

Here is a run-through of how each party can make money and benefit from the JV:

The Endorser: Takes a cut of the front end selling price of the product or service in return for introducing it to their customer lists. There is no fixed percentage but 50% is not unusual, and there are JV deals where the endorsers takes as much as 90% of the profits (or even more!). This sounds unlikely but can be done because the endorsee will make so much money from the back end and subsequent offers that they are sometimes willing to lose money on the front end in order to get that valuable customer name.

When making agreements with endorsers it is sensible to:

- Draft the contract from their point of view, ie. that they are the principal in the deal with most to benefit. If you use a standardized contract modify it each time you use it to reflect the specific needs of each endorser.

- Arrange for them to do as much of the endorsement as possible, ie. preparing sales material and sending it out. They will know their customers best, it avoids problems with confidentiality and also reduces your costs. This works best if you:

- Prefer an arrangement where the endorser takes the payment and sends the endorsee the order, together with their cut. This way the endorser is assured of transparency and is reassured that they will benefit.

The Endorsee: Takes a relatively small share of the profits – and in some cases even sells at a zero profit or even a loss. This might sound crazy but it is a proven strategy that does work. The profit is in the back end not the front end. Essentially the endorsee is buying new customers for a negligible upfront outlay.

When making agreements with endorsees it is sensible to:

- Ensure that they don't expect (or worse still need) a big upfront return.

- Ensure that they have a back end product/service or several back ends ready to roll soon after they have the new customer. The endorsee can then offer these products to these new customers and this is where they will make their money.

- Ensure that they are happy with the system whereby the endorser receives the order and the payment and passes it to them, with their cut. If possible, aim to reassure them by having some kind of affiliate or tracking program so that they can monitor the orders received by the endorser.

- Ensure that they will provide the same quality of product and service they do to their regular customers.

- Have a non disclosure agreement ready before you finalize any deals. Non disclosure agreements are contracts that ensure that any trade secrets that you share remain private and between you and your potential JV partners. More about this later.

The JV Broker: The JV broker – that's you – looks for potential candidates for deals and makes the introductions. They explain and educate both parties on what a JV is, and project the potential earnings. They might also help and advise with marketing. JV brokers can take a percentage of the profits from the sale and also from the commission too! That is, you might agree a commission from the endorser for their commission on the product they are endorsing, as well as a commission from the endorsee for all sales they receive from the customers they obtain as a result of the JV arrangement.

Tips And Pointers For Legal Agreements

It is important to note that the author of this book is not, his publisher is not and the distributors are not qualified legal professionals. You should always consult a legal professional before putting together any legal document or better still have them create it for you. The following does not constitute legal advice as we are not qualified to give it, please consider it to be general information.

Here is a checklist of some of the points you might want to cover in a joint venture agreement:

- The date on which the agreement begins.

- The date (or circumstances) on which the agreement will end.

- When and how the agreement can be terminated, other than at the end.

- How much commission is paid.

- Is commission paid after or before expenses are deducted, and what expenses may or may not be deducted.

- If a dispute occurs, which legal jurisdiction will it be resolved under.

- What rights does the broker have in representing the product and structuring deals.

- What formats can the product be sold under (ie. paper, electronic).

- Which parties comprise the JV (and which do not, eg. advertising agencies or the original supplier).

- Who does which tasks (eg. has responsibility for marketing the product, shipping, orders etc.)

- Other parties to which the list/product may not be offered, ie. competitors.

- Who prepares the marketing material.

- Who handles the mailings/e-mailings/e-zines.

- Does the JV broker have exclusive rights to represent the endorser or endorsee for a specified period.

- Whose website or other infrastructure will the JV be based on.

- Is there to be a ban on any unauthorized communications being sent to the list, including measures to ensure security and prevent spam.

- Level of access each partner (and the broker) will have to customers and sales information.

- A non competition clause, ie. that the partners (or the broker) will not start a competing business now or in the future.

Non Disclosure Agreement: Another aspect you may wish to include in your agreement is a *non disclosure agreement*. Alternatively this may also be dealt with as a separate agreement. A non disclosure agreement is used to prohibit sensitive information being released to parties outside the agreement, chiefly so that they cannot either undercut the agreement or duplicate the success of the JV with other parties.

So far as a JV is concerned it is often a good idea to use a non disclosure agreement to:

1. Restrict the financial details being revealed. It is often best that both the endorser and endorsee know as little as possible about each other's financial details.

2. Actual product details being revealed. This might also be governed by existing patents and copyrights.

3. Details of each parties' responsibilities being revealed and used, since this might be of benefit to direct competitors in circumventing the arrangement.

Getting Contracts: As we have already discussed, there is nothing wrong with drawing up and using your own letter of agreement. However, using an Internet search you may be able to find specimen JV contracts on the Internet. There is nothing wrong with using these as the basis of your own agreement so long as you check that they cover the points we have already outlined.

The Financial Aspects of a JV Deal

By this stage, you will need to negotiate the financial aspects of the JV deal.

This isn't the same as negotiating any other sort of commission-sharing deal. It is very important to note that it *isn't the same as an affiliate deal*, where the other partner might be happy with just a few pence per deal. This is one of the factors that makes IJVM more exciting and more profitable than affiliates.

In order to persuade your potential partners to work with you your offer has to be *better than average*. In other words give them a good, strong reason to work with you.

Nowadays you can get as much as 50% commission on some good affiliate deals. So don't think that prospective endorsers will be beating a path to your door if you offer them 'just' 50% commission on a JV deal. Some might, but deals for the best products and best lists with the best sales potential will rarely be done at this level.

For a real top quality, high profit deal you need to be thinking in terms of over 50% – perhaps 60%, 70% or more commission, based upon the profit margin of the product (not its selling price), being paid to the endorser by the endorsee. In some cases, in JV deals today, figures of 80% or even 90% are found. When you look at figures of that sort of magnitude you can see that very few prospective endorsers are going to fail to take your offer very seriously indeed.

In some cases, there are JV deals where the endorsee pays the endorser *100% commission* …. although it's normally on a limited number of sales, eg. the first 100 or 1,000 sales resulting from the campaign.

You might wonder how and why these sorts of figures are possible. But they are. Bear in mind that the endorsee would not make those sales in any other circumstances, so they really have little if anything to lose by offering such huge commissions. And there is the potential for generating massive amounts of profit from all the sales that result from the JV deal.

Your commission as JVB is based on a percentage of the profit made by both the endorser and the endorsee. (On some very favorable deals with a high profile and very successful endorser you might agree just to charge a commission to the endorsee.)

Of course these figures are examples only. You need to consider your product price, the profit margin the endorsee has available, and the selling potential of the endorser's list. But the message with successful JV deals is very much to think big, not small.

Example

When negotiating the financial deal you must remember that there are no set rules, and you should do what you must to convince both sides of the potential for this type of arrangement, even if that means you getting a smaller commission (which still could be a lot of money).

Let's assume for the sake of argument the endorser would get 60% of the profits and the endorsee 40%. Profit is usually defined as the money remaining after the cost of goods, the shipment of the product and order taking costs (0800 telephone calls, credit card charges etc.) and cost of advertising. Here's an example:

You are the JVB and you have an endorser that produces and sells financial courses. You also have an endorsee that produces and sells a study course in property investment. The course sells for £219.00. The production cost is £22, and shipping and order taking is £7, together totaling £29. The endorser has a customer base of 5,000 and in this case you decide to use a printed mailing, for which the cost is £3,000.

Your endorser (or your endorsee, or even yourself) agrees to pay for the printing and mailing of the endorsement. The endorsement is sent out and from the 5,000 customers, 500 order. 500 x £219 is £109,500. From that amount the person who paid to get the endorsement printed and mailed would get their money back. So we take away £3,000 costs from the £109,500, leaving £106,500. From that amount the endorsee would take out £14,500 (£29 x 500) as the cost of fulfilling the product, leaving £92,000 as the profit. From the profit everyone would get the percentage that they had agreed upon, e.g. the endorser 60% and the endorsee 40% …. and you get 40% of each party's take. So the endorser gets £55,200, the endorsee £36,800 and you get £36,800 (£22,080+£14,720).

The percentages will vary from deal to deal – and as you will see you could make a lot of money on much lower commissions than that – but the end result should always be a win-win situation for everybody. When everybody is happy the chances of undertaking another JV in the future with the same people will be high, and your endorser might become your next endorsee, and vice versa.

This is a win-win situation because:

1. **The endorser** gets profits from products they have not created ot stocked!

2. **The endorsee** gets profits from sales he would never have otherwise made.

3. **You** get profit just by putting these two parties together. You have no products, no fulfillment and no customer service issues!

Limited or Lifetime Commissions?

Another point to consider is whether you will offer your partners limited or lifetime commissions. Limited commissions are payable only for the specific campaign agreed upon. They are perfectly satisfactory for most agreements. Lifetime commissions are payable on all sales generated by a customer, for as long as they remain a customer. This means that the beneficiary can receive commission for many years hence, even for products and services that haven't been created at the time of the original agreement.

Although lifetime commission arrangements involve a long commitment and in some ways are to be avoided they can be a good way of attracting larger JV partners who might not be interested in a conventional deal. Note: Due to the complexity of tracking lifetime sales the endorser/endorsee will need some kind of tracking software (affiliate software can often do this) to keep track of lifetime commissions payable.

Summary

Constructing the JV deal itself is one of the most important aspects of joint venturing, and the area where the JVB does their most productive work. To make it a success, bear these basic tips in mind:

- You need a formal agreement, but creating a good deal for everyone is the best way to keep everyone happy.

- Small commissions (5%, 10%) aren't appropriate to JV deals – think big.

- The endorser gets the biggest share of the 'pot' in most JV deals – but the endorsee has much more to gain other than just the upfront profit. (So be sure to emphasize this.)

Joint Venture Marketing Techniques

(How To Make Your JV's Even More Effective!)

One of the great advantages of IJVB is that as a broker you are basically just an introducer. Once you've found a company with a product to sell, and a company with underutilized assets (e.g. customers) to sell to, you simply bring both parties together, let them get on with their business, and claim your commission.

However, to be really successful you shouldn't consider Internet JV's a totally leave-it-and-profit opportunity. There are JV's where this happens, and you would no doubt make some money, but you wouldn't truly exploit the potential.

For an IJV to be really successful it must be *actively promoted and marketed*. The good news is that you don't have to do all the work – the endorser or host does most of it. But as a good broker you also need to act as an *e-marketing consultant* to advise, assist and supervise to ensure they make the best possible job of it.

Bear in mind that even if your endorser runs a successful Internet business or is proficient at marketing they might not (yet) know much about JV's.

Another advantage is that, because you're working mostly on the Internet, JV marketing is also very inexpensive to do. Your endorser won't need to print lots of leaflets or run expensive ads. You do, however, need to have a strategy, deploy some effective techniques and target your marketing for best results. Also, just because e-marketing is cheap you don't want to use a 'scattergun' effect, marketing to people who aren't interested in the hope of finding good prospects. This might be regarded as spam and could jeopardize this and future JV's.

Crucial: The key to really successful joint venture endorsements is to have the endorser convey to their audience that they are genuinely trying to help them achieve what they want through their endorsement. They're not trying to sell them something …. they're trying to help them by tipping them off about this really neat product or service! And the beneficiary must make sure that they are offering a product which helps the prospective customer enjoy the same benefits.

Common Sense: Check periodically to ensure that your endorser's website is being well marketed and is well ranked – especially to make sure that its status hasn't changed since your initial research. This should ensure maximum exposure for your offer. (It also won't hurt to check your endorsee's website.)

Endorsement Marketing: Secrets Revealed

As we have said, endorsement is very much the secret of successful IJVB. Not only that, but it is vital to its success. The basic principle of endorsement is simple. It is essentially a recommendation from the list owner to his or her customers. But the more subtle you can be with your endorsement the better the results you are likely to obtain. In this section, we will examine the 'art' of endorsement more closely. You don't want to just wade in and say: "Buy This!"

Endorsing something is more than just advertising it. But exactly how do you get the balance right?

Think about this situation for a moment:

Imagine you are out shopping with a friend, or even a business colleague. You see them purchasing a product you perhaps haven't seen or heard of before – it might be a new cosmetic, a CD or a particular brand of beer. You've previously never thought of buying this product – perhaps you thought it 'wasn't you' or whatever. But they tell you that they think it's great, and they actually look forward to buying it!

You're impressed! As a result of that any considerations as to price, value or whether you really need it go right out of the window. You decide to buy the product as well just to see if it is as good as you say. That's endorsement marketing. You bought something as a result of an endorsement, even though your friend didn't actually try to sell it to you! Never at any stage did they scream "Buy this!"

This is exactly the sort of effect you need to recreate when you are involved in IJVM.

There are two forms of endorsement marketing: *Direct* and *indirect* and, in many cases, a combination of both.

Indirect

Personal endorsements can help sell the product – that's a fact. *If you utilize these in JV marketing they can be enough in themselves to persuade customers to buy.*

Endorsements should be either from people who are respected for their knowledge (experts) or from satisfied customers. For example, a doctor in the case of a medical product or a financial expert in the case of an investment product. Well known individuals are ideal, but even a recommendation from 'Joe Public' carries a great deal of weight.

So how do you get these endorsements? Your endorsee might already have some, if satisfied customers have written in with letters of thanks. Otherwise you can get them to ask their customers to do so. Another technique is to conduct a 'Customer Satisfaction Survey' and use the results.

If you want to get endorsements from known experts, arrange to send them a free sample of the product and ask them to comment on it. You may be pleasantly surprised at the level of response you obtain.

Paid-for endorsements are considered perfectly ethical. However, it is more professional to pay experts to give an interview or write an article than to pay them for their 'seal of approval'.

As you become more involved in JV's you will come into contact with many manufacturers, suppliers and retailers. It's quite feasible to ask them to endorse each others products even if they aren't involved in a related JV.

Direct

Direct joint venture endorsement marketing is where you arrange for someone to *recommend* the product directly to their customers, prospective customers or site visitors. On the Internet this is achieved by:

1. E-mailing information to their list of customers, or those who have registered with their website. Or:

2. Providing a link on the endorser's website to the endorsee's website. For best results the link should be to a mini-site exclusively for the endorser's customers rather than to a general site.

A simple way to achieve this is to set up an affiliate program for the product in question. Then when the endorser mails out their recommendation for the product potential buyers are directed via a special URL to a web sales or order page and the relevant commission can be distributed to the endorser (much higher percentages than an affiliate program remember). One of the easiest ways to set up an affiliate program, at least so far as digital products are concerned, is to use a service such as Clickbank (www.clickbank.com) to handle the sales. All the endorser needs to do is get a free Clickbank ID and you can then easily create the specific URL and the endorser can include it in the recommendation that they send out.

Great Endorsements …. And How To Prepare Them

Although actually writing the endorsement letter, mailing or other copy is the responsibility of the endorser the following sections will help you advise them for the best possible results because they may never have done this before.

The stronger the relationship the endorser has with their audience (list) the greater will be the response. If you plan on endorsing products through joint venture endorsement marketing you must build a strong relationship with your audience. Or, if you are working for the endorsee you must team up only with those who have a good relationship with their audience. **Most importantly, you must leverage off that relationship in the actual endorsement letter or script.**

If the endorser writes an obvious sales letter to their audience how is that an endorsement? How does that convey a genuine recommendation to them? Endorsements must be genuine. Otherwise, how will the endorser convince their audience that the reason for the endorsement is to benefit each of them, rather than to suit their own need to sell products and make extra profits?

An endorsement says: "Buy this great product from this other company, not from me." This has power, yes, but most people will think: "Yes but I bet you're making a cut out of it."

For an endorsement to work, it must blend in with the endorser's prior communications with the audience. A good endorser has a good relationship with their audience. This relationship is usually built by supplying helpful information to the audience. So, to make their endorsement blend in with their prior communications, their endorsement must appear as *helpful information* to them.

That's why the endorsement power of products is so much more powerful than merely sending out a mailshot package or even offering an affiliate program. Of course there is money to be made in affiliations but if your endorsee simply allows everybody and anybody to have affiliations with their website the audience will eventually have seen that endorsement over and over. In fact, the frequency with which customers are referred to the same website may actually count against it.

For any endorsement to be considered 'respectable' by the audience, it must show them a new value, resource, or make a special offer available to them. For example a special discount, two-for-one type offer, free services or extra guarantee benefits etc. It isn't special to offer your endorsement customers the same offer that is available to everyone else. When a really special offer is made, the recipients of the letter do not consider the endorser to be a seller, but rather their own special 'deal hunter'.

More Types of Endorsement

Endorsement literature often reflects the foundation on which the endorsement was arranged. The foundation means the 'reason why' the endorser chose the endorse the item in the first place. In this respect there are mainly two types of endorsements. All endorsements can usually be placed into one of the following two categories:

Free Information/Resource Endorsement

Free information/resource endorsements are probably the easiest to get on the

Internet by far. By creating an online infrastructure that supplies helpful information, publishers (whose job is, after all, to supply useful information to their audience) will feature in some aspect of your infrastructure (or that of the endorsee).

This aspect is usually something that supplies helpful information like a discussion board, e-zine, helpful website, article etc. These are all kinds of media that supply people with helpful information that can be used for back end marketing.

There are three main reasons why publishers make free

information/resource endorsements:

- To meet their obligation of supplying helpful information to their audience.

- For reverse exposure.

- For a cross endorsement.

Understanding the concept of reverse exposure can make you a lot of money in IJVM. Reverse exposure is when a publisher endorses your infrastructure to their audience but that publisher is also part of your infrastructure.

For example, you may be using a discussion forum. You invite several publishers to participate at your discussion forum. One of those publishers participates and then announces your discussion forum to their own audience. When they do this they get their audience to go to your discussion board. Not only do the audience members gain helpful information at the discussion board itself but they see the 'helpful' posts left by that publisher and their loyalty through the endorsement value is massively increased.

Below is an example of a free information/resource endorsement. In this case, the endorser was asked by the broker to visit a particular website and discussion forum. Suitably impressed they made this endorsement to supply helpful information to their audience of over 50,000 subscribers. The endorsement was made by means of an article entitled 'How To Turbocharge Your Website'. They gave six steps to e-marketing including –

- be personal,

- generate publicity,

- use advertising, add links,

- articles, and

- encouraging participation in the online community.

They explained each step and then their endorsement of the

discussion forum was made in the 'participation' section:

PARTICIPATION: Taking part in online discussions and forums is a great way of getting publicity. These boards are also great places for learning from the experts in this business. Visit Fred Smith's new board and you'll see what I mean. You'll find it at www.???????.com. And what a top site. Have a look around before you leave. Other leading discussion boards are listed in my article on....

Notice how this endorsement is part of the article. <u>It doesn't seem like an advertisement in any way, shape or form</u> – but of course, it is!

Product Endorsement

Product endorsements may be a bit harder to obtain than free resource endorsements although it depends on your particular circumstances. However product endorsements bring in more cash more quickly.

Product endorsements are usually made in one of the following situations:

- For reverse exposure.

- To introduce a new value or special offer which is exclusive to the audience whereby the audience respects the endorser for making the endorsement.

- With the aim of developing cross endorsement.

- On a per-order commission basis.

When writing product endorsement literature you must concentrate on how you can make the endorsement appear <u>as editorial material rather than sales copy</u>. This is harder to do in a product endorsement than a free resource endorsement. That's essentially why you need to make a special offer to the endorser's audience.

Caution: In IJVM one of the easiest ways to fail with an endorsement is to endorse a product which can be bought at a well known affiliate site. Everybody knows (or will soon realise) that it is an affiliate site available to everyone and that you haven't arranged a special offer just for them. (If, however, you do want to set up your own affiliate program for some reason try to disguise it. Use a CGI script that creates affiliate versions of your URL which use real names rather than obvious affiliate numbers.)

Try to come up with plausible reasons to explain to the reader why you are making the audience, not selling them something. You can use reasons like these:

After reading this information and trying the product, I couldn't help but pass this on to you.

I was looking for a bargain for my customers, and here's what I found ....

I can't help sharing this with you. This is brand-new, and I wanted to let you know before everybody else finds out.

My friend told me about this.... I couldn't believe it at first, but when I tried it out it worked! Now, let me tell you about it.

One of my long-time colleagues contacted me the other day. After talking with him for a while, I convinced him to share these secrets with me ....

A friend I know in the ??? business just began stocking a new product ....and after trying it out, I immediately contacted him to see if he could make it available to you, my customer. And I'm delighted to tell you that not only did he say 'yes', he's set up a very special offer for you too!

Endorsement Mediums

You can carry out JV endorsements through a number of different mediums. This includes mail, fax, e-mail, phone, by using e-mail bulletins and e-zines or adding endorsements to websites. In each case you should try to choose the ones through which the endorser comes in contact with their customers, clients, or subscribers most often. Your endorsement script or copy will also vary depending on which medium you choose.

Here's an example of an e-mail one JV broker provides to an endorser:

Dear ???

You're one of our most valued customers and we'd like to suggest a new product to you. I should tell you that we don't actually stock it, but a good friend of ours does. It's a terrific product and we're guaranteeing you'll like it. Just the thing for busy people like us!

Oh and there's another thing. We've arranged for you to try it out without risk. We can even have our colleague send it to you and he won't bill you until you try it for a month. If you don't like it, all you'll have to do is give us a call, and we'll see to it that it's picked up .... and you won't be charged a penny!

Why not take a look? It's here .....

Here, they make a special offer by allowing the customer to try it for 30 days before purchasing. Most importantly, they take away all risk. In your endorsement letters, tell the prospects that if they don't like the product, you (or rather the endorser) will personally see to it that the company benefiting from the endorsement gives them a money-back refund.

In many cases you don't even need to negotiate these special offers and extra value. The endorsee will already be willing to provide them as part of their existing sensible marketing strategy. All you need to do is just fine tune the offer, personalize it to your own customers, and see that it is well promoted in the copy.

Better Marketing Support Means Higher Sales

Here's a useful checklist of some marketing materials you might prepare and give to your endorser, or assist them with:

- ⁻ ☐Pre-written mailing pieces.

- ⁻ ☐Pre-written e-zine ads.

- ⁻ ☐E-zine articles with links pre-inserted.

- ⁻ ☐A unique domain name just for them which directs people to the endorsee's site.

- ⁻ ☐Free e-books or reports for distribution, or links to where they can be downloaded from.

- ⁻ ☐Access to a banner library.

- ⁻ ☐HTML web pages which they can host on their own domain, with redirection to the endorsee's website.

- ⁻ ☐MP3 audio files of information that 'soft sell' the product.

- ⁻ ☐HTML code for pop-ups, pop-unders and slide-in web pages that promote the product.

These items can all be provided on a CD, or set up on a download area from your own website, if you have one.

E-Zine Promotions And JV's

One of the simplest ways and most potentially powerful ways to make money from JV's on the Internet is to ask e-zine publishers to review your partner's product and to include that review in their e-zine. This is already extremely big business in the USA, where there are already thousands of e-zines, and is sure to be equally popular in the UK and worldwide in due course. If your partners already publish their own e-zines or electronic newsletters then this should be one of the first areas you consider for collaboration:

This technique can be extremely effective. However, the catch is that you have to make sure that your product is very targeted to your audience. E-zines tends to be very specialized to their subject. For example, a car e-zine would normally not just be devoted to cars or even a particular make of car, but an actual model of car (perhaps even a specific year model!). So any endorsements carried in that e-mail would need to be targeted precisely at owners/enthusiasts of that model.

You should make this kind of deal as attractive as possible to the endorser – ideally 60% or more commission, plus some free products to give away as a promotion if possible.

Here are some specific techniques for e-zines:

Ad. Swaps: Combine several e-zines together into an advertising package. Endorsees can then access regular exposure in a number of different publications.

Cross Recommendations: Arrange with a number of e-zines for them to carry a 'Recommended e-zines' section in their publication, in which each other's e-zines are recommended.

Product Endorsement Swaps: Arrange for endorsement messages to be carried in e-zines on a reciprocal basis.

E-Book Promotions And JV's

Here is a very clever way of generating a never-ending stream of JV partners. It is also a way to find endorsers for almost any endorsee who won't charge you a penny commission for recommending your product for you. It is a kind of viral marketing and isn't strictly a pure JV marketing technique, but can be incredibly powerful.

This can be achieved by writing your own e-books then giving them away, together with rights for others to give them away. The e-book itself contains endorsements which are carried throughout all the complimentary e-books generating, potentially, millions of leads over the years! It is, in practice, a secret JV sales force working for you!

Look at it this way: If you publish an e-book on your endorser's website (or even your endorsees) and 10,000 people download that book. And then just 100 of them publish it on their website, or give it away, with 5,000 downloading it from there. And then some of them publish on their website. You can see how this could mean hundreds of thousands of what are essentially free endorsements.

This method is particularly well suited if you are working with e-books, but you do not have to be. It will work with any product area where information is part of or relevant to that product. You don't even have to create a lengthy, full-blown e-book. Even a simple report will do the job – if it is something that a lot of people are going to be interested in and the information is truly valuable.

If you have a knack for writing then you can easily write your own e-book. If not hire a freelance writer. (By giving them an endorsement in the book you could even set up another lucrative JV!)

Here's an example of how this type of project might work: Assume you are arranging JV's for gardening websites and products. A simple e-book passing on gardening tips – or even a series – along the lines of 'Grow Better ....' would be easy to write and very popular and could lead to hundreds of thousands of downloads over the years, each carrying your endorsement message.

The Importance of Tracking Orders

Once you've set up a JV deal it's very important that you can track the orders that result from it. This will allow you to see how effective (or otherwise) the deal has been, and also to ensure payment of the necessary commissions.

In conventional marketing it is easy to track orders. If it's an endorsement in which people can order by mail you have a code on each order form. If it's an endorsement in which people order by phone you need to have people dial or ask for a certain extension or person. This is called keying. You can key response and orders to/from Internet based offers in much the same way, except that it is a little more technical.

If customers are ordering by website you can use one of the tracking programs which are available. If you are working with a JV partner who doesn't know how to do this there are a number of services available on the Internet.

Boosting Your IJV With OFFLINE Joint Ventures

Although Internet JV's are designed to be conducted on the Internet – thus benefiting from the speed and low cost the Internet offers – there can be many advantages in joint venturing with offline businesses both as endorsers and endorsees, but particularly as endorsers. The main one is that you can reach target audiences (for your endorsed product) that it is difficult or even impossible to reach using the Internet. Since most IJVB's don't even consider offline activities it can also give your brokerage an additional tool for success.

The key to successful JV's with offline businesses is to find ones that have exactly the same target audience – regardless of the fact that they are marketing or selling offline. For example, if you're looking to sell travel insurance you wouldn't want to set up a JV with toy shops, but you might set them up with travel agencies, airlines and so on.

Here are five ways to exploit offline opportunities:

1. Write a tip booklet related to the business being endorsed, which includes an ad. for your endorsee's website, which your offline partner can give away. For example, a garden center could be given tips booklets relating to a gardening website.

2. Create printed flyers advertising your online partner and give them to your offline partner in order to hand out. In return your offline partner gets an ad. on the website.

3. A good way of incentivizing this is to print the flyer on bags and packages – so the partner gets a free product.

4. Get your offline partner to include an ad. or recommendation for your online partner whenever they advertise in the press, or even on TV/radio.

5. If your offline partner carries out direct marketing, has a regular newsletter, a privilege club (by which regular customers receive periodic special offers) etc. examine ways in which you can participate – perhaps even paying part of the costs in exchange for advertising opportunities.

The Importance of Building Relationships: A Reminder

Whenever you are involved in the promotion of JV offers don't forget the importance of *building relationships.*

The more technology enters into marketing, the more relationships are important. Otherwise, you become just another website. Just another sales letter. Just another ad.

It is crucial, in joint venture endorsement marketing, that you build relationships – not only with other business owners, but also with your customers, subscribers, or other audiences. Offline collaborations are a good way of fostering relationships within your IJV.

Deal Boosting Tips

- Ensure that your partners pay out commission fully as agreed, and on time.

- Once you have completed a successful IJVB deal ask the other parties involved to write you a reference or letter of recommendation. If everything has gone well they will probably be more than happy to do this for you. You can use these documents in persuading more parties to let you set up a JV deal involving them, or even to attract new partners.

- Always treat your JV partners with respect and professionalism, be honest and upfront at all times. Remember in a joint venture you are instilling trust with one another. If you agree to promote your partner's products or service, make sure you follow through on your commitment.

Top JV Marketing Blunders to Avoid

IJVM is 'failsafe' marketing much of the time. If your endorsement comes in the form of a genuine recommendation, with special offer, made to qualified customers who you know are interested in the product in question then, most of the time, you shouldn't fail to make sales. However it is possible to make a few mistakes. These occur either due to unfamiliarity with the product or, often, over-enthusiasm for an opportunity which can lead to pressing ahead without really thinking it through. In this section we will look at some of these common mistakes, and how to avoid them:

Insufficient Familiarity With The Product

JV marketing is often used with highly targeted customers who will know the product very well indeed and any unfamiliarity, or errors, may be easily spotted. It is always best to work with partners selling products with which you are familiar yourself – ideally you should use them yourself. This makes it much easier when dealing with the endorser and the endorsee, and also helps when preparing marketing literature.

In some cases it can be a positive disadvantage to be unfamiliar with the product: And if you don't use it yourself because you think it is 'junk' or 'too expensive' then ask yourself why anyone else should want to buy it either! And why are you wasting your life promoting it? Just for the money? Come on!

Poor Quality Products

All the exciting possibilities of JV deals sometimes disguise the fact that some products are just downright poor. So try to look behind the potential and at the product itself. Is it good quality? Is it price competitive? What other alternatives are available? What sort of service does the company offer?

If you choose a poor product then not only can your JV project founder, but it can affect the credibility of your future JV deals as well. Don't be afraid to 'pull' JV arrangements where customers raise any significant quality concerns.

Dubious Testimonials

Customers can be skeptical about Internet testimonials because it so easy to fake them – and it often occurs. So you need to be scrupulous about any testimonials you are given to use by the endorsee. Check them out, and ensure that there's a real person behind the name. (If you don't, the endorser and customers probably will and your deal will be wrecked if they turn out to be false.)

Although testimonials are not strictly copyright it's also sensible to ensure you have permission to use the testimonial from the original writer.

Excessive Use of Banners

Banners are easy, cheap and very tempting to use. But don't rely on banners to promote your JV offer. Apart from the fact that consumers are becoming used to ignoring banners they don't carry sufficient weight.

Remember that the whole efficacy of JV selling is that you are endorsing a product not advertising it, so your endorsement should be written into the website as a news or advisory piece and preferably couched in personal terms. Banners don't do this, and just leave people feeling they've been sold to and shouted at.

You might consider using a banner as a supplementary method – to make it convenient for the buyer to buy – but only in a limited way. Purpose designed banners are better than banner exchange stock.

Interference From Affiliate Programs

Affiliate programs aren't the same as JV arrangements. Affiliate programs simply don't have the same power that the personal endorsements in well created JV programs do. So, beware setting up deals with companies or sites where the affiliate program is allowed to dominate the site – usually because the owner believes it is an easy way to profit (which it isn't). The JV endorsement is the main profit center and should be given absolute priority.

This isn't to say that affiliations can't co-exist happily with JV's. However, they are best used as a source of back end profits, after the initial endorsement has done its job.

Overlooking The Benefits

A common mistake with JV endorsements is to forget that the objective is to sell. The best way to sell, as agreed upon by marketing gurus worldwide, is to push the benefits to the customer. Some JV endorsements forget this and instead focus on how good the *endorsee* is – an easy mistake to make when preparing material of this type. But this can cause the response to fall well below that which should be expected.

Consider the difference between the following two pieces of copy:

The Best Copywriting Course On The Web

(Bad Endorsement)

And:

Increase Your Profits By 200% With The Secrets You'll Learn In This Copywriting Course

(Good Endorsement)

Not Knowing Your Target Audience Adequately

If you don't know your target audience it's very difficult to sell them. So you must know, or get to know, the people who will be buying whatever your endorsee will be selling. Find their wants, needs, desires, tastes, fashions and motivation – and write that into all your endorsements.

If possible spend some time with your target audience. Set up a focus group, or at least conduct some interviews – by telephone or even e-mail.

Flea Market Sites

Your endorser might have an impressive looking site, but is it a *flea market site?* In Internet terms, a flea market site is a site with no particular theme – it has a bit of this, and a bit of that, but no single strong theme, interest or product area. Flea market sites are often easy to spot because they have links to other, totally related and diverse sites.

To sell really successfully with a JV arrangement your site needs to be well focussed and single minded. This is the only way to pull in sufficient visitors with enough interest in whatever you're talking about. Flea market sites can't offer you this kind of pinpoint accuracy. In these cases you'll need to spend some time with your endorser to iron out the problems with their site

Lazy Partners

Lazy partners are prospective partners who think that JV arrangements (and even affiliate programs) are an easy way to make lots of money without doing any work. They aren't of course. Lazy partners think it will be easier to sell someone else's product than their own. They also tend to get involved with lots of programs (including affiliate programs) and don't stay with any of them very long.

When you approach a new partner try and consider how enthusiastic they are, and try to assess if they think, wrongly, it's going to be money for nothing.

Dull Sites

Sites that are dull and boring, no matter how solid they are, tend not to make very good partners for JV arrangements. Always visit the sites you're thinking of partnering with extensively, several times, and if they don't interest and excite you there's a possibility that other visitors won't be excited by them either. If you find a site with potential that is slightly dull then work with the site owner to enhance their site.

More Marketing Options For JV's

Here are some more ideas you can use to make JV marketing even more effective:

- Organize back end offers.

- Add cost-sharing, or ride-along participants.

- Offer free gifts (to entice both JV partners and customers).

- Interviews with one or more JV participants published on the website or in an e-zine etc.

- Joint authorship of products (books, e-books, newsletters, e-zines, columns, articles, guides, directories, brochures etc.).

- Monthly automatic subscriptions for products which can be supplied regularly (for example, nutritional supplements).

- Point of purchase endorsements.

- Product or service upgrades.

- Profit related to volume levels achieved.

- Deals enhanced with some immediate profit potential for one party (maybe even 100% of the profit for a one time deal) to close the deal.

- Multi party deals involving more than two JV partners.

- No obligation trial periods for customers.

- Yearly contracts to provide services.
  Co-operative advertising, where a number of JV partners share the cost of advertising one partner's products in different media (press, radio, TV) on a rotating basis. The

leads generated are then shared amongst all the partners.

- Simple link exchanges with more partners.

- E-zine ad. swaps.

- E-zine column swaps (partners write a regular column for each other's e-zines).

- Ride-alongs. Mailings for the other partner are sent with direct mailings.

Sample Letters

Letter One: Sample JV Proposal Letter

Dear (Insert Name)

(If you don't know their name put Sir/Madam)

We work in what is the fastest growing business development opportunity on the Internet. Since you seem to be doing very well with your site –

(Write a few words about their site)

– we want to share an idea with you which we believe will make you a fantastic extra profit, while also providing a very valuable service to your customers.

We represent a product that is a wonderful, much needed (but non-competitive) product your customers will love. So confident are we in this product we're prepared to meet all the costs …. and accept all the risks!

If you're interested please call me one day this week, and I'll explain everything in full. It will only take about ten minutes of your time …. but it can mean thousands of pounds to your bottom line!

I think you'll be as excited as I was when I found you on the Internet. So don't let this opportunity pass you by …. give me a call today.

Yours Sincerely

(Insert Your Name)

PS. If you prefer I can call you. Just reply to this message with your telephone number and a convenient time to call and I'll be in touch.

It really is as fantastic as it sounds. All you have to do is endorse this product to your customers and share the profits. It's so simple and – yes – it works!

Letter Two: Sample JV Proposal Letter

Dear (Insert Name)

I have a great proposition for you!

I am currently promoting (Insert Product or Service) and I would like to propose a partnership that will make us both a steady stream of income. (Insert Product or Service) is very hot right now and with the excellent commission (?% – ?% recommended) I am able to offer you there is a lot of potential for the both of us.

I have sales materials ready for you as well as links to track your commissions. If you are interested, send me an e-mail and I will send you a free (Copy or Trial) of (Insert Product or Service) so you can examine the fantastic potential of this product yourself.

I look forward to hearing from you soon. Please take a moment to review the enclosed sales literature, or visit our website.

(Insert Website Address)

Best Wishes

(Insert Your Name)

Letter Three: Sample Endorsement Letter From The Endorser

Dear (Insert Name)

A couple of weeks ago an estate agent called me and started telling me about a Property Investment Course that he's developed. Now I've seen my fair share of these courses so I really wasn't that excited. He was excited though, so I asked him to send me a copy of the course.

A week later I received it. It didn't seem really special from the simple packaging, but I opened it up and decided to take a quick look at it.

My 'quick look' actually lasted into the early hours. Needless to say, that was some of the best property investment information that I've ever read.

So the next day I rang him and asked him to tell me more. He told me that he was selling this course for £199. I told him that I wanted to let a select group of my customers in on it, but that there was no way I could do this unless he was willing to give them a good deal.

After some haggling back and forth he agreed to reduce the price to £167 and add in a manual and video that he normally sold for £99 about buying repossessed property at a fraction of the price. I checked the video and manual out and they were excellent.

With that bonus included, I thought that this would be a perfect package for you. So he sent me some more details, and I've attached them for you.

If you've ever considered investing in property I would *highly* recommend you get this course.

Oh, I almost forgot. He also promised me that if you weren't 100% happy with the course, you could send it back within 60 days for a full money back guarantee! You can't say fairer than that.

So, as always, I wish you the best and if there ever is any way that I can be of service, feel free to contact me.

Kind Regards

N E Endorser

PS. Even though I had convinced him to give you the manual and video package free, he promised me that he can only guarantee this bonus until (Insert Date) or until stocks run out.

Send a sales letter like the one above to the endorser's customers, and you can be sure that everyone in the deal will be satisfied!

Examples of Joint Venture Marketing Partnerships

- Book club/travel companies.
- Bookshops/publishers.
- Business success book seller/business success seminar giver.
- Car insurance/car dealerships.
- Cosmetic companies/health clubs.
- Car accessories/parts store/car dealership.
- Car insurance company/car accessories vendor.
- Charity needing donations/virtually any type of company.
- Computer hardware dealers/computer software dealers.
- Construction firm/architect/interior designer/landscaping firm.
- Credit card company/holiday tour operator.
- Estate agent/removals company/home insurance/mortgage company.
- Film developer/camera retailer/travel agency.
- Graphic designer/printer.
- Grocery stores/cookbook publishers.

- Gyms/private health insurance.
- Insurance salesperson/financial consultant.
- Landscaper/lawn care service/plant nursery.
- Law practice/financial consultant.
- Newspaper or magazine/mail order company.
- Petrol/gasoline retailers/motor insurance.
- Plumbing services/electrical services.
- Printer/designer.
- Radio/TV station/virtually any type of business.
- Removals company/packaging store/storage facility.
- Resort hotels/airlines.
- Software developer/Internet service provider.
- Software company/e-book publisher.
- Travel agency/car hire.

Profile of a JV in Action

Let's say you're interested in sport and, using your research, you locate a company that specializes in selling sports and leisure wear. They have a website and undertake other marketing activities, including direct mail to which they receive approximately a 2% response .... with which they're quite happy.

Now let's say you identify another company who supplies footwear by mail order, including a range of all the most popular trainers, football boots etc. at competitive prices. You approach the sportswear firm and structure a deal where they would contact their customers with an endorsement of your other partner's footwear – including special price, delivery and guarantee options for their customers.

The result? The very same offer that is normally sent out to the footwear company's mailing list is sent out to the sportswear company's mailing list – together with a personal endorsement letter from the proprietor. But, this time, it pulls a 15% response!

The beauty of joint venture marketing is that not only can one company have their product or service endorsed by someone else to their customer base, but the reverse can be undertaken too. Not only does it produce a massive increase in sales, but the customers who receive the endorsement are even grateful to the endorser, generating even more customer loyalty for them.

What happens when you've fully exploited that mailing list? No problem! Just find more companies to plug into the joint venture. For example, suppliers of event tickets, sports coaching courses, corporate hospitality, medical insurance, physiotherapy and all kinds of outdoor pursuits clothing could all be linked up into the same JV's.

In each case, as a joint venture broker, you find a company that has an established customer base, and that has a relationship with those customers that is positive and healthy. Your first job is to contact the potential endorser and educate them about the resource that cost them the most to acquire, yet is being tremendously under used – their customer base.

Your next job is to find a specific product or service that you think the endorser's customers would be interested in. Once you've located the product, you contact the product owner and in turn would introduce them to the power of endorsement marketing.

In turn for you arranging the JV deal you would get a 'piece of the pie' from the endorser or the endorsee, or possibly both.

50 Benefits of Joint Ventures And Joint Venture Marketing

We know that, after reading our manual, you will already be convinced by the power of JV's. But you can use this list of 50 benefits to help you sign up your JV partners!

1. You can build profitable long term business relationships.

2. You can increase your credibility by teaming up with other good businesses.

3. You can get free products and services.

4. It costs virtually nothing to set up a deal.

5. You can get new customers, or new leads.

6. You can get discounts on the products and services you need.

7. You can cut your operating/marketing costs.

8. You can out-compete your rivals.

9. You gain referrals from other businesses (for nothing).

10. You can make your business simpler.

11. You can save time.

12. You can get free advertising.

13. You can keep your customers longer by offering them free goods and services.

14. You can prosper through slow periods of the year.

15. You can share advertising/marketing and save – or stretch your budget.

16. You can enter new markets.

17. You can grow your business quicker than otherwise.

18. You can acquire new skills.

19. You can improve your cash flow.

20. You can find new profit centers.

21. You might become rich!

22. You can start complete new businesses this way.

23. You can sell slow-moving or unwanted stock.

24. You can reduce your debts/overdraft without increasing your spending.

25. You can reduce your prices – and so sell more.

26. You can enhance your e-commerce activities.

27. You can get free marketing help/advice.

28. You can outsource some of your work …. for free.

29. You can unlock hidden sources of income.

30. You can swap poor product lines for good ones.

31. You can widen your funding options.

32. You can (in some cases) save tax.

33. You can open up new distribution channels.

34. You can reward your staff better.

35. You can improve your personal life – more money, less work!

36. You can increase your sales and benefit from economies of scale.

37. You can build e-mail lists that work.

38. You can save on employee time/costs.

39. You can build your own e-mail opt-in list for free.

40. You can cut competition as firms who would have been competitors becomes allies.

41. You can learn insider secrets from other businesses.

42. You can test your product for nothing!

43. You can outsell affiliate programs.

44. You can attract more interesting, more lucrative business offers.

45. You can offer more bonus products and incentives.

46. You can get endorsements and testimonials for use in all your marketing.

47. You can increase your e-zine/newsletter subscribers massively.

48. You can under price your competitors.

49. You can find new products to sell, and increase your back end activities.

50. You can create new products fast.

Useful Websites

Automated Software Search Programs

Copernic: www.copernic.com

Website Research Services

InterNIC: www.internic.net

Network Solutions: www.networksolutions.com

Uwhois: www.uwhois.com

B2B Mailing Lists

Business Lists UK: www.businesslistsuk.co.uk

Business Lists USA: www.infousa.com

Website Directories

DMOZ: www.dmoz.org

Yahoo!: www.yahoo.com

(Yahoo! operates as a 'website directory' rather than a conventional search engine.)

Forum Directories

Hyperboards: www.hyperboards.com

InvisionFree: www.invisionfree.com

Cross Promotion Forums

Business Exchange: www.cashconnection.com

eBay (Not strictly a JV information source, but good for contacts): www.ebay.com/community and www.ebay.co.uk/community

Business Directories

Kellysearch: www.kellysearch.com

Thomson Local: www.thomsonlocal.com

Yellow Pages UK: www.yell.co.uk

Yellow Pages USA: www.yellowpages.com

Newsletter & E-Zine Directories

E-ZineHub: www.ezinehub.com

List City: www.list-city.com

The Zine & E-Zine Resource Guide: www.zinebook.com

The biggest e-zine article site: www.ezinearticles.com

Order Tracking Systems

The CGI Resource Index: www.cgi.resourceindex.com

Please Note: Websites included in this section, or elsewhere within the manual, are all operational at the time of writing and we do aim to check and update these listings on a regular basis. However, due to the nature of the Internet and the way in which websites can appear and disappear without notice it is always possible you may find some sites which have been renamed, moved or removed. If you can't find the information you require using one of these contacts then running an Internet search using your favorite search engine will usually produce all the contacts you need for IJVM.

7 Secrets of Web Wealth

"Many Chatter About Wanting to 'Get Rich on the Internet' But Not One Person in a Million Knows The REAL Secrets of How To Do It..."

It should keep you awake at nights. It should cause you anxiety and unrest. It's the knowledge that thousands of ordinary men and women are getting quietly wealthy from the Internet – and YOU aren't!

These people are working less than half your hours and making ten times the money.

They are, in the main, one person operations – usually the whole 'empire' is run from a PC in a spare corner of the room. There are no customers to visit, no sales calls to make, no hard work. Yet for every one of these successful people, there are at least one hundred 'dabblers'. Those who have a half-hearted 'go' at a web site and then moan to all who will listen that it didn't work for them and they never made a single sale.

Where are they going wrong? The answer is simple – they focus on just ONE success factor (e.g. the product) and ignore the other six factors. The truth is, if you want to make a killing on the Internet there are seven cogs you need to assemble into your money machine. Miss one or miss-align one and that machine will remain jammed solid or spin its wheels pointlessly. Either way, no money comes out. There is one big difference between the winners and losers – the winners are willing to learn how to do it right. The losers never study success and lack the energy to create such a money machine. Which are you? Presented in this amazing Blueprint is the distilled knowledge of the Internet gurus who have made hundreds of millions between them. Read. Learn.

Apply!

Would you like to make £100k+ a year from your PC in under an hour a day, running a highly profitable internet business? There is surely more misunderstanding and myth surrounding this than any other area of business. People get this *so wrong* – when getting it right is easy. Stuart Goldsmith reveals the secrets others are charging £5,000 a time to learn. Now at last you can claim YOUR share of those Internet millions! Read on to discover the Seven Secrets of the Internet Millionaires.

There's a question I'm asked so often it drives me crazy.

It's this: *"How can I get rich on the Internet?"*

It's a good question – and I know the answer – or rather, the answers.

In this very special Blueprint I'm going to attempt to give you the set of 'golden keys' to Internet wealth. I will distil the knowledge which others are selling for £5,000 a pop. **Contained within these few pages is the 'secret knowledge' about how to get wealthy on the Internet.**

It's not hard – but you must know how to do it and follow the system. Deviate from this path and you will almost certainly fail.

An all too common thing I hear with regard to making money on the net is "it can't be done". This comment is nonsense, so please put aside any negative thoughts and doubts which may hamper you.

Saying this can't be done is akin to saying nobody can make money in business - and you know that isn't true (I hope!). You see, the Internet is in effect Yellow Pages on amphetamines.

That's all it is.

The Yellow Pages is widely accepted as an excellent way for a business to get customers because people who go there are clearly in the market for something. The difference of course is the 'on amphetamines' part. The Internet is more sophisticated than

Yellow Pages, but once you get your head around the concept, you'll find it very easy to understand.

No-one is a special case. No-one. ANYONE can tap into this amazing source of wealth and I intend to show you how in this blueprint.

The Most Important Web Wealth Secret

Let's say you and I are about to compete against each other with a Hot Dog stand each.

What advantages would you like to have?

Take a minute now to write down what advantages you'd like in order to out-sell me. Very important - think about this before continuing...

Ready?

OK then. What did you decide on?

Some extra-yummy buns? The world's best selection of toppings and relishes? How about a really cool-looking stand which glimmered in the sunshine? Or maybe the hot dog sausages themselves are the best in world - real frankfurters imported from Germany? Maybe you'd like to be cheaper than me?

Whatever you chose as an advantage, I will grant you. In fact, I'll let you have them all just so long as in return, you will grant me the <u>one</u> advantage I want…

Fair enough? Good.

Because I will wipe you out with the thing I want in a single day!

What is it I want?

A queue of really hungry people!

Get the point?

You focused on PRODUCT and you LOST.

I focused on MARKET and I won. End of contest.

Would it matter if I didn't have all the relishes, yummy-buns and imported frankfurters? No! In fact, even if my hot dogs were expensive and mediocre I'd still have beaten you hands-down!

Let the market drive you is the point I'm making. The days are gone when you wake up and decide on a neat product and wonder if you can sell it. You should be asking: "Is there a market *already* and can I reach it?" That's the important question.

This is why I'm a Direct Marketer (Internet marketing is one type of direct marketing). I am entirely market-driven. I only hit 'starving people' - people who want certain things. I let them TELL ME what to sell them and that's the most amazing thing about the Internet - the guesswork is over because we can clearly know where the 'starving people' are.

I want you to go back now and think long and hard about the little exercise we just did because if you can get your head around it, you will have put yourself in the top 5% of business people in the world. I guarantee it!

The vast majority of companies are what's called 'product-lead', meaning they think of a product and then think how the market fits in with their schemes.

That's all back to front.

Their energies are all centered around finding the right product, when they should be centered around finding the right market. This is an important distinction and is not splitting hairs.

People also ask me: "What should I sell on the Internet?" Answer: That's the wrong question! It takes your attention away from the important question, which is… "*How* can I sell on the Internet?"

So in case you're thinking: "What can I sell on the Internet?" The answer is: It doesn't matter. You can sell safes or Elvis memorabilia; Sindy/Barbie dolls or trampolines; haunted portraits or vintage microphones. The product is almost irrelevant.

Marketing is everything.

So if you have ever – even in a small corner of your mind – wondered if you could make a living, or even a fortune, from a web site, this Blueprint is exactly what you need.

Here's the first secret and the place where most people stumble before they've even tried. There is no single answer to the question of making money on the Internet. To make a great living or make your fortune you need several elements which are put together like the cogs of a fine machine. Miss one element, and you won't ever get that money machine ticking no matter how furiously you crank the handle.

This is why 99.99% (yes, really) of web sites make no money. This is why almost all *how-do-I-make-cash-on-the-web* questions are wrong – because people are asking just <u>one</u> question when they need to ask seven.

What I'm about to reveal is worth thousands upon thousands of pounds to you.

Okay, let's get started…

There are 7 secrets to web wealth and I'm going to give you them all here in a single document. But before I do, please let's get the stage clear of clutter.

I am NOT talking about a web site as an adjunct to a flourishing company. For example, a nationwide swimming pool installation company with a thriving TV and press advertising campaign which also has a web site. Yes they may make sales from their site, but the site is not what's really doing the selling. Their other adverts do that.

I'm talking, mostly, about the one man or one woman lone entrepreneur who wants to make a tidy living, in their spare time, from an odd hour or two on their PC. Their web site is their primary selling tool. They have no brochures, leaflets, TV slots or full page adverts or direct mail campaign. It's the housewife, taxi driver, teacher – anyone who wants to make decent extra cash in their spare time.

I'm not talking to thriving, existing businesses here (although they may learn something). I'm talking to small scale start-ups.

Are we on the same sheet of music? Great. You're about to learn what very few people know…

Secret #1 What Product to Sell

I'm starting with this because I have found from bitter experience that I cannot get onto the real secrets of web wealth unless I address this question. People are obsessed, consumed and laser-beam focused on this one question. They think that once they know the answer, their golden ship will come sailing into the harbor.

It won't. Making fantastic cash from the web has got virtually nothing to do with the products you sell.

Surprised? It's the truth.

All we care about is the market and the marketing methods. Get these right and the profits will take care of themselves.

So all I'm going to do is give you some pointers on product. First you've got to be keen on what you sell. Ideally you should be fanatical about it – but maybe that's too much to ask. **You can't sell stuff you don't believe in.**

Next, we're looking for niche markets here, not vast worldwide markets. We're not selling cola, cars, mobile phones, trainers, TVs, shampoo and suchlike. Those are for the Big Boys. We, I humbly submit, are not Big Boys and Girls, we're amateur small fry. Is that okay with you? So because we are small fry, we have neither the financial resources, nor the clout to sell 'to the world'. So we don't try.

We want niche markets but… (get this) **with enough people to**

have continual ongoing sales. Heck, if you could make a grand a week, I'm guessing you'd be a pretty happy bunny, right? So we're not talking mega deals here. But too small a niche won't work. I once new a guy who hand-made wooden propellers for vintage aircraft. I mean, come on! He must have spent some

lonely days waiting for the phone to ring! That's WAY too small a niche.

Next your product must be easy to mail or deliver. Downloads are perfect (e.g. software or information products) because your shipping costs are zero. But failing that, ideally go for smallish, lightish things which can be popped into a jiffy bag and mailed out. This is not a hard and fast rule. I mentioned safes earlier because I once knew someone who sold them by mail order!

I'm a huge fan of information products because they are easy to ship and have no quantifiable 'real' value (is a manual worth £200 or just the paper it's printed on? It depends on the content!). If you love golf or have some inside knowledge about something you'd like to share, great! You might even want to write your own material if this was the case.

And don't think there won't be a market for it! Just take a look at this website:

http://www.keyworddiscovery.com/

Enter a word or phrase and you'll see how many people search for it each month on the Internet. You'll also see all the various sub-categories of that word or phrase. Play around with it - it will open your eyes and it's an incredible marketing tool in the right hands.

Clearly, we want to cast a line into the lake with the most amount of fish in. So as well as doing something close to your heart, I also recommend targeting people who want health/wealth/happiness. They are a large market and hungry for products too.

There must be a thriving market in what you are selling. This means you are unlikely to be the first into the market and you are unlikely to have something totally unique.

This is GOOD, not BAD. We don't like to be first, nosiree. We like to enter markets thronging with punters all hot for the sort of product we want to sell into that niche. We want a packed market of Elvis enthusiasts where we set up store with our niche market in Elvis tea towels.

KEY CONCEPT: Your aim as an entrepreneur, is to find a MARKET, not a product. Find some hungry fish, THEN find some food for them.

This makes things easy, not hard! Once you find the market, there shouldn't be a question about whether your product will work. It's more like: "How *much* will they like it?"

The companies which embrace this simple concept become huge successes. These are the companies which are centered around the market. By the same token, companies which center around a product do poorly or fail.

When a business fails, all number of lame excuses are offered, when in fact the REAL reason is almost always that...

...THEY DIDN'T SELL THINGS PEOPLE WANTED TO BUY AT A PRICE THEY WANTED TO PAY!

If you have a business already, or even if you work for someone else, take a look at that business now and ask if it is product-centered or market-centered.

Every single enterprise you embark upon should be based on evidence that a particular market wants something you can provide.

Also, remember that marketing rewards reality not ego!

If there are vast piles of money to be made from penis enlargement pills or diet schemes or baldness cures (and there is by the way) and you sell them, marketing will reward you.

Don't even think about a product until you have the market, then make the product fit the market.

You're not even going to create a website until we have found the MARKET!

Are you seeing a pattern here...? Market, market, market. The 3 keys to making profits with ANY business, not just an Internet business, but on the Internet, NEVER BEFORE has this concept been more crucial to grasp as you will see here.

That's all I'm going to say on product.

Secret #2 What Should Your Web Site Look Like?

People get this one absolutely 100% totally wrong!

As a 'one man band' they think they must project the image of a large, multinational corporation to cover up for the fact they're running off their kitchen table, so they strive for home pages which look like this: http://www.bbc.co.uk or this: http://www.ibm.com

Ugh. This could not be further from the sort of thing we want. We are NOT a large corporation, we're trying to sell stuff not project an image. We are lying when we set up a corporate front end because in reality we're running from a bedroom. It fools nobody. Worse than that, it damages sales because (and this is a HUGE secret) the people in our marketplace **want to buy from real people, not faceless corporations.** They can get that in the High Street. By going corporate you are destroying your largest advantage which is that you're a real, honest to goodness person.

Your web site has one main purpose (and one only) – to sell stuff. So folksy, honest, simple and direct are your watchwords.

Corporate, slick and glitzy are your enemies. It's also a giant ego trip to go 'corporate'. It makes little old you feel like a big, powerful organization. If you're in this for the ego trip, fine, just don't expect to make any money!

So to be absolutely clear, here's what to avoid…

Logos.

Drop-down menus.

Fancy graphics.

Animations.

Sound.

And the good news is – that makes them cheaper to create! In fact the sort of web site you ought to be creating should cost no more than £250 - tops

Now I'm a great fan of text-driven web sites. That means sites which have a text-only sales message. Very few graphics are involved with the exception of:

1. A product shot if it needs one.

2. A head and shoulders shot of you, the honest-to-goodness proprietor. (Not in a suit please. Make it a warm, 'I'm a normal bloke/woman' sort of shot.

That's it. No other graphics or pictures.

Here are some great examples of text-driven sites. And hey they sell a shed-load of stuff, so maybe that tells you something?

http://www.billfryer.com/copy/

http://writingwithpersonality.com/

http://www.overnight-copy.com/

http://www.copywritingthatsells.com.au/

http://smallbusinesscopywriter.com/index.html (not as 'clean' as the others, but still good.)

http://www.tinawrites.com/

Interesting that those sites are all done by top-gun copywriters, isn't it? In other words, **they're created by people whose job it is to sell stuff on a daily basis.**

And you *are* interested in selling stuff, right?

Ten Golden Rules For Killer Web Sites

Here are the golden rules they won't teach you anywhere else:

1. NO LOGO! Nobody gives a monkey's about your logo apart from you. It's an ego trip. Dump it.

2. Mainly text.

3. No graphics. No animations.

4. No menus if possible.

5. NOTHING which leads them away from the text of your message.

6. Your sales message (the WORDS) are what carries them through to the sale at the end.

7. Neutral background.

8. Not full width lines – too long to read. Tiring.

9. Two colors maximum.

10. Black ALWAYS for the 'body text'.

Secret #3 Who Should Design Your Web Site?

Answer. Not you.

Okay, with one exception – if you're a professional web site designer I'll grudgingly allow you to do it.

Otherwise, please do us all and yourself a favor and put away your FrontPage and any other web design software you have invested in. Here's why:

You don't know what you're doing, and... you don't have the time to learn it and... it costs loose change to have someone do this stuff for you.

Analogy: Your plumbing goes wrong now and then and your fuses blow now and then. So why aren't you squandering your irreplaceable life mugging-up on plumbing manuals and electrician's handbooks? Answer – life's too short. You'll make a hash of it even with some knowledge because it takes years to learn this stuff, and when you need this work doing, you call in the pros and slip them a couple of hundred.

So why, on God's green earth, are you futzing around with trying to learn web design? Stop it immediately! Hire a pro. But not any old pro. 'Web Designers' are ten a penny. Most of them are housewives with 5 hours experience on Microsoft Frontpage who do a bit of 'web design' in between the supermarket run and picking up the kids in the 4 x 4.

Now I want to take a step back to basics for the benefit of the large number of readers who know what a huge opportunity there is on the Internet, but, by their own admission, haven't a clue about where to start and/or think they need a degree in computer programming.

The good news: you don't need anything of the sort!

I have a confession to make: I really don't understand the technical aspect of the workings of the Internet *all* that well...but it doesn't affect my Internet profit opportunities one little bit.

I do all my work through a web-master (a techie). I leave it to the professionals.

But here's something you must know: **A web-master is basically your translator.**

They are NOT experts at Internet marketing - they are technical people. You communicate to them what you want your website to look like and other things like auto-responders. They can set everything up for you; everything from the domain registration right through to your website design and customer response mechanisms.

Forget technical knowledge - you don't need it. The applicable word in the phrase "Internet Marketing" is MARKETING.

Making money on the web is not about techie stuff - it's about making money in a business by applying the time-honored principles of marketing.

Here's what you do – find a web site you like, locate the designer of it, and hire them. If you can't find or get them, keep going until you get another one equally as good.

What else?

Oh yes, you need to keep your web designer on a tight leash. You see… they're *designers*. And you know what they're like. Serious "lovies" given half a chance! There's nothing they enjoy more than a good chat about pantone colors over a china cup of chamomile tea. They also love the technology, so if you leave the 'arty' door open even a crack, they'll be in there with graphics, sound clips, flashing banners and the works. Let's face it, they're bored rigid by the sites I mentioned earlier. "What? Just text on a neutral background? Aw, come on, please can I slip in some neat animated graphics? They're such fun to code…"

The other thing they don't like is the bill they can slip you. Because our sites cost about a third as much as the sites they'd like to create. You know, the sites which sell nothing but look good?

I admit some sites need to be a little more complex, so here's an example from the masters of marketing, Agora. http://www.earlytorise.com/. But don't go any more corporate than that – and then only if you have several products to sell and/or you have a lot of information to impart.

Secret #4 How Many Products Should You Sell?

Simple. One.

Next question…

What? You want more? Sigh...

When you are starting out you need to find a niche and find one product (or a tiny range) and concentrate 100% on selling that. Sell Elvis Tea Towels (but not also Elvis records and Elvis autographs). Sell a squirrel-proof bird feeder (but not also garden gnomes and hammocks). Sell a home cure for athlete's foot (but not also cures for dandruff and nail fungus).

You want an example?

I thought you might. You're in for a treat because I want to reveal to you a masterful site, one which you should look at, gaze at, lovingly stroke the screen. It is perfect. It is a masterpiece. When I'm alone at night, I turn on my PC and just gaze at it… (hmm... maybe I should get out more...)

It sells one product and does it EXACTLY how you should do it.

Check it out:

http://www.thecureforathletesfoot.com

Whoever put this site together is a master.

They totally understand web marketing and how to sell stuff. Please use this site as your template, your bible, your instruction manual. Once you 'get' this, you will never again be uncertain about how to sell on the web. When you have a designer, just point them to this site and say "That's what I want, now go to it you camomile-sipping arty-techie type and none of yer lip…"

Secret #5 *Why* Do People Use The Internet?

Think for a moment. Why do YOU use the Internet?

If you're struggling, let me help you. Do you go on the Internet because you want stuff sold to you?

I submit the answer is no, not very often.

So why do people use the Internet?

There are two reasons: To check email and search out INFORMATION.

If people are taking the time to go into a search engine to find something out, don't you think you can profit from this? Of course you can! This is the very essence of successful Internet marketing.

Let me prove this point to you:

Why has Google (www.google.co.uk) become THE search engine of choice?

Take a look at their home page and tell me…

How different is it to say, www.msn.com?

Yes, it is devoid of banner ads!

People using the Internet don't want to be sold something; they want information…and THEN end up actually buying something if there's no heavy sell. You MUST get your head around this because when you do, you'll be poised to scoop out your share of Internet profits.

So that means your web site should have a certain amount of 'take home' information which addresses the customer's need, and then gradually build up to a sale.

The standard formula is 'headache – aspirin'. The first part of your pitch talks about their 'headache' and sympathizes with their problem and offers some practical guidance and help (that's the take-home content). The second half builds to a gradual sale of the 'aspirin.'

That's a really important gem.

Secret # 6 The Landing Page and Credibility

KEY CONCEPT: Internet businesses which fail ALWAYS do so for 2 simple reasons:

1) Not enough traffic being driven to the website.

2) The traffic being driven to the website is not converted into a sale effectively.

It's that simple! There is no mystery here- every problem boils down to one of these two factors.

IF you have a product which is in demand (and you can prove if it is by using http://www.keyworddiscovery.com/ remember?), the success of your Internet campaign is down to these 2 simple factors: driving the traffic and converting it.

So let's talk about driving that traffic first.

A website is like Las Vegas without the casinos!

Have you been to Vegas or seen a picture of it? If so, you'll see that it's just a big city in the middle of the desert. And yet, every day thousands of people fly into that city. Why? Because of one extreme pull factor. Gambling.

Now, I'm going to explain something that virtually no beginner to Internet business understands…

If all you do is put up a website and expect money to magically pour in somehow you're effectively expecting people to fly to a city in the middle of the desert just for the hell of it! I promise you, it won't happen.

You have to *drive* the traffic. Give people a burning reason to visit your particular area of desert.

So okay, just for a second then, let's imagine we *have* driven traffic to a website. Now we have to make those visitors to our website want to buy, right?

Sounds obvious? Then how come so many Internet entrepreneurs only talk about 'hits'. Or put another way, how many *visits* this website or that website gets. Imagine if you tried to judge the takings of Las Vegas casinos by the number of passengers getting off the planes at the airport! That would be crazy. None of them could spend a dollar, or all of them could spend a million dollars each. We can't judge from the arrivals figures.

So let me put a myth to bed finally about Internet marketing: HITS are completely irrelevant; SALES are what we're concerned about. Are we actually making any money?

Remember this - HITS stands for "How Idiots Track Success"!

So what we're going to work on now is converting hits into sales.

Show me the Money

The very first web page the person you've directed sees is something called 'The Landing Page'. Most Internet marketers make the classic mistake of not paying special consideration to this landing page.

The landing page is the first thing the visitor sees. The most important thing to remember here is **not to confuse the visitor or scare him or her off.** What would confuse them or scare them off?

A perceived inability to fulfill their need.

KEY CONCEPT: Remember why your visitor came to your site in the first place. Think about the process which got them there. What KEYWORDS did they enter? They have a problem they want to solve, so they entered a keyword in a search engine or responded to a small classified advert or an email advert in an opt-in ezine. They saw your pay per click ad and clicked on it. And now here they are on your landing page.

If you've got them this far, now's the easy part - just show them how to solve their specific problem with your product/service. The landing page has but ONE task and that's it.

Does the visitor want or expect to see a mass of flashing lights, banner ads, links etc etc? NO, NO, NO.

Think back when we considered why Google had become the search engine of choice. Because it was an uncluttered page designed for just one thing - to find information required to solve a problem.

Ask yourself this important question about your landing page: "What ONE thing do you want your visitor to do and how can you get them to do it?"

Do you want them to subscribe ('opt-in') to your email list so you can send them a free newsletter (which sells other products) perhaps, or go straight for a sale? In both cases, give the visitor no-strings information which moves them closer to their goal (and ultimately leads to a sale).

It's very important to make the landing page as relevant to the visitor as possible and totally uncluttered. With that in mind, you should have a separate landing page for each category of customer rather than some sort of menu where they have to select it themselves.

KEY CONCEPT: Ideally, the visitor should see the keywords they entered in their search as much as possible on the landing page. If they went to a search engine and entered "Athlete's Foot", they see your website link and then click on it, don't you think the customer would like to see those same words straight away on your website when they get there? Something like:

"At Last, a Fast Cure For Athlete's Foot That REALLY WORKS!"

Of course! They want immediate confirmation they've come to the right place. Sow how come the first thing most people see is a fancy logo, banner adverts, a bewildering series of drop-down menus, tabs, a riot of colors, flashing graphics. In short, general bewilderment. Here, in my view, is a classic example: http://www.888.com/

This stuff isn't complicated if you think about it. And remember, you just instruct your webmaster to do all this.

I will now reveal something which most net-entrepreneurs still haven't figured out about the Internet - even large corporations (especially large corporations actually!). There are 2 things the Internet is starved of:

- Informational Content
- Real Contact

If your website can fill this void you elevate it above all others.

Let's look at each in turn…

Remember and understand something: people use the Internet predominantly to GET INFORMATION. <u>So provide it</u>!

Yet this is just some of the irrelevant garbage people put on their websites…

- Meet the team; our history; our products; our industry awards; news of our new building; get on our mailing list…

Me, me, me…that's all the visitor is interested in, *not* you and your company, your building, your awards and your 'team' or your fancy logo. <u>They have a PROBLEM to solve</u>. If you had terrible toothache and turned up at the dentist, would you be interested in meeting the team, admiring their logo or looking at their shiny awards?

There's another CRUCIAL aspect to converting hits into sales. Something becoming increasingly important on the Internet:

CREDIBILITY

Thanks to the media working everyone into a frenzy over a few scammers on the Internet, people have become paranoid about ordering on the Internet. So if I had to pinpoint one massive advantage you can give yourself for zero cost it's this:

Make your phone number clearly visible!

This is important. If there is a *real* phone number which allows the visitor the option of speaking to a *real* person, prominently located on the site, much of their fear will dissipate. Take note!

"What, give out my phone number so that… customers can… *gulp*… call me with their orders and queries?"

Yes! If you want that huge advantage I mentioned. You CAN cower incognito behind a faceless site – if you want virtually no orders that is! By the way, you will be surprised at how few people call you - but what enormous confidence it gives your buyers.

Secret # 7 Driving Traffic to Your Site

Okay so how do we get people to visit our site, once we have set it up in the way I have explained?

Here are the 6 ways we can achieve this:

1. Pay for an advert (like a Google Adwords) to appear on peoples' searches. 'Pay per click.' For example, if you search under my name, Stuart Goldsmith, you should see that my own web site comes at the top of the list – that's because I pay for it to do so!

2. Manipulate the search engines so that our website gets in the top spots for FREE when people search for something. This is also called "Search Engine Optimization" and it's why you need a decent web designer and not Glynis Jones from 43b, Ruby Terraces who's doing it as a little hobby. Your web designer will know exactly how to get your web site as close to the top of the search engines as possible. This takes more time (often several months) than buying your way in – but it's free!

3. Tiny adverts in classified sections of newspapers. These are low cost, simple adverts which contain a headline and a web site address:

Athlete's Foot Cured?
www. CureAthletesFoot.com

(I just made that web address up, it's probably in use but I haven't checked.)

4. Create your own opt-in ezines which has solid information but also has slots for adverts. This is a little known secret of the Internet millionaires. It sounds a lot of hassle but it isn't really – and you end up with that most valuable of things, an opt-in email list of your own. See later for more tips.

5. Put those same adverts in other people's opt-in ezines. They will want a cut of your profits of course.

6. Send someone an email which persuades them to go to your website. This is Email Marketing, not SPAM.

Now, when I mention 'email marketing' to anybody, the first word which enters their heads (because the media told them so) is "SPAM". Let me make something crystal clear from outset: **I hate Spam with a vengeance...**

You know how the ridiculous spam email goes: "Hey, Mr. Goldsmith I noticed you have not yet tried Cialis (A Viagra substitute)! You have never been a real man in bed until you have!" Just like that, but with all kinds of weird spelling and punctuation. Great... like even if I WAS in the market for such a thing, would I buy it from a monkey like you? A monkey who makes me feel inadequate and insults me?

Yeah... right.

I get about 20 of these things a week, do you? And you can't unsubscribe either. Imagine the postman tying to deliver you a letter you don't want - you tell him you don't want it, but he forces his way through the door and rams it in your face! Is that marketing?

Spam is the most low-life, lazy-bum, idiotic form of marketing I've ever seen.

Let me qualify what is meant by 'spam' because there is much confusion here. **Spam is an unsolicited email trying to sell you something you have never expressed the slightest interest in buying.** By 'unsolicited' I mean, you did not agree to be sent any emails from the party in question. Obviously, that is unethical on their part, but most of the time, what people think is spam, actually isn't; they just forgot what they agreed to 'opt-in' to!

Most email marketing is sent out by an 'autoresponder'; this is basically a computer which is able to send out large quantities of emails at a time.

So by making that definition clear, I hope you appreciate something: **NEVER, EVER SEND OUT SPAM!**

Great. So how can we legitimately use emails to drive traffic to our site, or more specifically, traffic which will actually BUY SOMETHING from our website?

There are 2 ways:

    1.   Email list rental

We use only opt-in email lists: This would be where you rented the email list from a company which has its own email list of people who apparently asked to receive emails on a certain topic (e.g. health). Most of the time, these lists are very unresponsive as the people who are on them usually just forgot to untick a box somewhere in the small print and ended up on the list. When they get an email they think they're being spammed (even though they're not really). Double opt-in list rental is slightly better. This is a better quality list to rent and quite rare. This is where the person has been put on an 'opt-in' list but also, they have been sent a confirmation email which asks them once again if they want to be sent email messages. So they have in fact opted in twice. However, there's something even better than this...

   2.   Your own list

This is the best one of all. What your ultimate aim in all this should be is to build your own email database of customers as quickly as possible. Your own email list know you and trust you (providing you've earned that trust).

So how do you drive a customer to that website via an email?

The first and foremost factor is getting them to actually open the email in the first place! You've done it yourself when you check your email; you try to spot stuff you're not interested in quickly so you can delete it right? So the key is making sure the subject of your email looks interesting and the reader can easily see it's from you.

Why should the reader care if it's from you? Because you're about to be one of the very few people who actually understand email marketing. It's all to do with this simple secret:

Give and ye shall receive!

<u>At least</u> 50% of the emails you send out to your email database should NOT be selling anything!

Yes, you did hear me correctly. It's all about give and take. Here's the analogy: Are you a beef farmer or a dairy farmer?

Both farmers have cows, but they use them very differently. Now, is it best to slaughter your cows for a quick buck or to keep them alive and milk them so you can reap profits indefinitely by providing them with goods and services which will really benefit them?

I hope you would agree the dairy farmer is the most sensible. The only catch with that is, he has to keep feeding those cows or they won't produce milk. But it's a price worth paying.

So what am I saying here?

If all you do is try and sell stuff to your email list, you might make a quick buck, but you will soon have no email database... because you'll be the first email they delete when they check their inbox!

"Oh, it's that guy trying to flog me something AGAIN... delete!" Remember, people don't really like to be sold anything. Enough said.

So instead of selling the living hell out of your list when you get it, keep feeding them with freebies. Whether it's a free report occasionally, a mini-course, a manual, a newsletter or just some juicy titbits. Do so without trying to sell anything (ghost writers can produce all number of freebies and special reports if you don't want to do it, but it could be a simple tip from you about something). They'll be looking for the catch - surprise them by there not being one! Do you think they're going to delete your email next time? Maybe, but at least you're in with a fighting chance of them opening it.

Your email database should be considered your most valuable treasure. You should make it a top priority to create one. Nurture it. Build a rapport with it. Most importantly, don't rent it out and don't spam it!

You should make a concerted effort to 'train' the people on your email database to OPEN your emails.

How do you do this?

By making them realize that more often than not, YOUR emails represent something of VALUE... for NO COST!

Common sense right?

Questions

Before I end, here are two other questions I'm often asked:

"What about tax?"

What about it? Pay it! There's absolutely no point in concerning yourself with issues like this until you actually create an income to pay tax on! Your company structure would ideally be a sole trader or an off the shelf company you can buy for £65 and which can be set up very quickly and cheaply on the internet (just do a search on 'company formations'). Appoint an accountant ONCE you have some money coming in, not before.

"Won't someone copy my ideas?"

What makes you think you need an original idea to make good money? <u>You don't</u>. There are very few genuinely original ideas - most businesses are based on re-packaged ideas from someone else. Like the tax question, making money and having someone copying your ideas is better than making no money! **Get in the game, then worry about things like this.** Don't use these minor details as excuses to prevent you from having a go.

I don't blame people for being negative; not many people make money on the net… that's because they don't understand it. And like anything we don't understand, the temptation is to 'poo-poo' it like a petulant child.

The internet is separating the winners from the losers in marketing and this is a HUGE opportunity for you - the fact that not many people 'get it' yet. A look at what passes for web sites will convince you that most people haven't a clue.

In time, everyone will look back and wonder what all the confusion was about, but until then, a few people (you) can greatly capitalize.

Why shouldn't it be YOU who creates an automatic, turn-key, low risk, high-profit internet business? And when I say 'automatic', I mean it. Once this is all set up, there's really very little work to do. The key is to get it set up properly, following these seven secrets.

Okay we've covered a huge amount of ground in this blueprint and I honestly think this is arguably the most valuable 12 sheets of paper you could ever own. Please keep it somewhere safe to refer to time and time again when you set up websites.

I hope you agree that nothing I've said here is rocket science. How can it be? Tens of thousands of very ordinary people are making fantastic money on the web – they've all grasped these seven secrets and put them to work. Many of them paid a LOT of money to learn these secrets in seminars given by the top Internet gurus.

Now it's your turn!

I hope YOU become the next Internet millionaire.

www.ingramcontent.com/pod-product-compliance
Lightning Source LLC
Chambersburg PA
CBHW051320170526
45166CB00002B/620